North-South Technology Transfer

Financing and Institution Building

Jack Baranson
Developing World Industry and
Technology, Inc.

Lomond Publications, Inc.
Mt. Airy, Maryland 21771
1981

Library of Congress Catalog Number: 81-80543

ISBN: 0-912338-27-X (Clothbound)
0-912338-28-8 (Microfiche)

Printed in the United States of America.

Composition by Barbara McGiffin.
Jacket design by Markey Graphics.
Printing by BookCrafters, Inc.

Published by
Lomond Publications, Inc.
P.O. Box 88
Mt. Airy, Maryland 21771 U.S.A.

PREFACE

The crux of the problem in the field of technology transfer between U.S. and Latin American enterprises is the ever-widening impasse that has resulted from the growing gap between Latin American demands and the inadequate supply response of U.S. enterprise groups.

This book addresses this problem. It is an outgrowth of a study that was funded by the Office of External Research of the U.S. Department of State, entitled, "North-South Transfer of Technology: What Realistic Alternatives Are Available to the U.S.?" The original study was based upon field visits by the author in 1977 to each of the three countries analyzed in separate chapters—Brazil, Mexico, and Colombia. This material has been supplemented and updated through previous and subsequent visits for the design of new financial mechanisms to support the technological upgrading of industrial enterprises and supporting institutions in each of these countries.

The background to the studies, and related efforts on which this book is based, concerns the continuing set of issues between the United States and Latin American countries over the international transfer of industrial technology and U.S. business enterprise involvements in Latin American countries. Many of the problems and issues exemplified in the three surveyed countries apply in varying degree to other Latin American countries and to newly industrializing nations generally.

At issue is the basic conflict between emerging national objectives in Latin America and elsewhere to utilize the technology factor as a pivotal element of national economic growth and development and segments of U.S. business enterprise which feel harassed and threatened by the new policies and their impact on commercial operations in these countries. In particular, U.S. firms with equity investments or licensing arrangements object to what they consider as infringements on their industrial property rights and upon their latitude to manage commercial operations. All three countries surveyed have pressed for the "restructuring" of the technology transfer environment at both the national and international levels. Along with most other developing countries, they are seeking to establish an internationally binding code of conduct to govern transnational enterprise relationships.

The tendency in this area of controversy has been to engage in mutually incriminating and often acrimonious dialogue, rather than to seek positive and mutually advantageous solutions. Part of the problem lies in a failure on the part of the United States to fully understand and appreciate the new set of development policies underlying the drive toward greater technological independence and self-sufficiency. On the Latin American side, there has been an unwillingness to accommodate to the commercial realities relating to the management of technology assets from the supplier's viewpoint.

Commingled with the commercial considerations of U.S. enterprise are broader questions of U.S. international trade and technical assistance involving its Latin American neighbors. These economic and political considerations must also be factored into adjusted relationships based upon a new parity of interests and objectives. The alternative is to run the risk that the perceived impasse between U.S. commercial and economic interests and Latin American national development goals will deteriorate into mutually destructive political and economic confrontation. The way lies open for the United States to reformulate its trade and commercial relations so that they continue to benefit segments of the U.S. economy, while at the same time respond to the emerging aspirations and perspectives of Latin American societies.

In Mexico, there is the background problem of illegal immigration into the United States, spurred by high levels of chronic unemployment and the management of Mexico's newly developed energy resources as leverage in support of national technological development. In Brazil, the concerted national effort toward progressive technological development is symbolized in the U.S.-Brazilian confrontation over nuclear energy, in contrast to opportunities for mutually advantageous technical and commercial development of gasahol from agricultural raw materials. In Colombia we also find, on the one hand, analogous effort by governmental authorities to gain fuller control over the technology factor in the management of energy and mineral resources—and the challenge posed to U.S. business interests. On the other hand, there is the opportunity for cooperative U.S.-Colombian enterprise-to-enterprise efforts in the energy field and in support of Colombia's national efforts to improve the productivity of its country's urban and rural poor.

This book provides a comprehensive examination of the technology factor in national economic development, as exemplified in the three countries surveyed, and the measures undertaken in each to enhance their technological absorptive and self-generating capabilities. In each country study an examination is made of the extent to which technological development needs have been served through traditional enterprise-to-enterprise transfers. The case materials contain some of the innovative arrangements that have been negotiated with U.S. enterprise. Both the case materials and the analytical framework should prove useful to scholars and teachers in the field.

Our overview and analysis of the shift in Latin American policies and of the new types of arrangements that U.S. firms are entering into should prove useful to involved segments of the U.S. business community and in the formulation of U.S. foreign policy toward Latin America. The enlarged demand for industrial technology on new terms, coupled with continuing efforts by Latin American economies to expand exports of manufactured goods to the U.S. and other world markets, poses new challenges for adjustment and accommodation between U.S. policy regarding domestic production and employment and international relationships with newly industrializing nations—particularly with countries like Brazil and Mexico that are in the vanguard of industrial progress and leaders in developing world efforts to change the international economic order. Our study provides some insights and recommendations on the nature and direction these adjustments and accommodations might take, based upon mutual interest and advantage. Our analysis of technological absorptive capabilities and implementation mechanisms in each of the surveyed countries is intended as background to the proposed mechanisms, as is the diagnosis of constraints in the supply of technology on the U.S. side. These proposals should be of direct interest to policy makers in both the United States and in Latin America, and of general, prototype value to other industrial and developing nations.

I wish to acknowledge the contributions of Anne E. Harrington, who carried out part of the original field work in Mexico and had a major role in the analysis and preparation of the country studies in the original research. Richard Dana updated certain background material in the country chapters. Nancy Barax prepared and proofread the index.

Dr. Jack Baranson
President, Developing World
Industry and Technology

CONTENTS

Contents

LIST OF FIGURES

CHAPTER I
OVERVIEW OF PROBLEMS AND ISSUES

THE TECHNOLOGY FACTOR IN LATIN
AMERICAN DEVELOPMENT

Within the more advanced countries of Latin America, a new set of policies has emerged with regard to the technology factor in national development, and a new attitude toward multinational corporations has ensued. These policies focus on rapid industrialization based upon a new and revised access to foreign technology and rapid growth of internationally competitive domestic industries. Technological self-sufficiency has become a primary goal in many of the newly industrialized nations' development plans, and the strategy toward that end encompasses the progressive transfer of engineering and management capabilities, rather than technology embodied in plant and equipment. Latin American development authorities are now keenly aware that the key to long-term growth and development lies in acquiring the ability to design and engineer industrial systems, which in turn necessitates the development of indigenous capabilities in product design, process engineering, and equipment design and construction.

There are several reasons for this new orientation in development strategies. One is that Latin American economies have reached a stage of development where industrial enterprises need to achieve substantial increases in productivity and competitiveness in order to sustain continued growth. Industrial plants in Latin America, producing largely for tariff-protected, domestic markets, have been heavily dependent upon foreign licensing sources for technology, resulting in product designs and production systems that rarely are competitive in world markets. In the seller's market that generally prevails in protected economies, product designs and production techniques are often stagnant and lag behind in terms of improvement and modernization.

The aforementioned tendency is intensified by the privileged position of subsidiaries of foreign firms and large national enterprises, both of which have easy access to packaged industrial technology, including trademarks, patents, processing techniques and equipment, and a full range of technical services and managerial systems. In addition, foreign-owned firms are often able to bypass technology payment restrictions

---

*A list of abbreviations will be found at the end of the Chapter.

that smaller, local firms are unable to avoid, thereby placing the latter at a competitive disadvantage. State-owned enterprises in Latin America also have much less difficulty in the technology acquisition area, since they have access to the financial resources and managerial talent needed to choose and negotiate for technology, whereas smaller Latin American firms encounter difficulty even in searching for appropriate technology and in arranging for suitable adjustments in product design or purchased processes and equipment.

Latin America has been especially critical of foreign-owned and controlled subsidiaries that bring with them industrial technology and thereby obviate the need for developing indigenous design and engineering capabilities or supporting capital goods industries. Once established in an economy, foreign-based multinationals also preempt or stultify the development of indigenous industry because of their comparative advantage in management and technology.[1]

Technological upgrading is needed especially at the domestic enterprise level to meet increased competition at home and abroad. Technological upgrading involves new and improved products and product designs, new and improved equipment and processing techniques, the use of new and improved materials, and the introduction of new and improved production methods. In some cases, this may involve more dynamic and aggressive licensing arrangements, which break the dependent linkages with single licensing partners, and move on to more diversified sources of equipment, materials, product designs, process licenses, and hired technicians. A principal inhibiting factor has been the lack of financial resources and mechanisms to fund the purchase of technology from foreign sources and/or to obtain indigenous design and engineering support services. Improved access to technology sources and design-engineering resources can contribute significantly to increased productivity, an extended utilization of domestically available energy and mineral resources, and an enhanced competitiveness in world markets.

ROLE OF INVOLVED COMMUNITIES IN NATIONAL TECHNOLOGICAL DEVELOPMENT

Increasingly Latin American nations have resorted to interventionist efforts to restructure the demand for, and supply of, technology in their respective national economies and in the world economy at large. Programs and initiatives have related to each of the four functional sectors—(1) government, (2) financial, (3) science-technology, and (4) business enterprise. Each of these communities impacts upon the transnational transfer and domestic utilization of technology. The nature and efficacy of involvements understandably vary from country to country depending upon the involved mechanisms and programs, and the skills and capabilities of involved people and institutions. The country chapters on Brazil, Mexico, and Colombia contain sections analyzing the relative function and role of each of these communities, as follows:

1. Restructuring supply of technology (*screening* and *control*).

2. Restructuring internal demand for technology (*planning, searching,* and *negotiating*).

3. Reinforcing the absorptive infrastructure (*training, supporting, using,* and *generating*).[2]

Until recently, most national mobilization efforts in Latin America fell within the first category. Initial strategies to restructure the supply of technology were aimed at an international level and focused on obtaining international consensus on a Code of Conduct which would be binding on the actions of multinational corporations. This strategy also sought major revision in the international property system which, in the Latin American view, placed them at a disadvantage in acquiring foreign technology. Failure to obtain cooperative support in this strategy, particularly from the industrially advanced countries, led the developing nations to incorporate these legal and regulatory changes into their respective national laws regarding foreign investment and technology transfer. All three of the countries surveyed have instituted programs to restructure the supply of industrial technology to domestic enterprises.

MYTHS AND REALITIES CONCERNING TECHNOLOGICAL DEVELOPMENT[3]

Certain misconceptions concerning the nature of industrial technology and how it is derived must be dispelled if we are to deal realistically with the problems of technological development in Latin America and the related set of North-South technology transfer issues. To begin with, science and technology cannot be packaged like any other commodity and dispersed by the industrially advanced countries along with their other foreign aid. Science and technology do not come in convenient, self-contained units that can be packaged and shipped for use from one part of the world to another. Technology is derived from a continuum of activities encompassing research, development and engineering, which in turn is often intimately linked to ongoing production and marketing activities. Most industrial change—which includes the design and engineering of the products themselves, the materials that go into them, the equipment that is used in processing materials, the work methods and management control systems—is a continuing process consisting of a myriad of elements which results generally in small incremental changes. The diverse "products" of science and technology activities are derived from often unique social environments. Technology "products" are further linked to user environments that provide the signals for what is needed in the way of new or adapted products or processes.

Another basic misconception is that dependence on foreign technology may be substantially reduced or eliminated through the development of indigenous science and technology in universities and research laboratories. In reality, the extent to which technological self-reliance can be achieved depends in large part upon the stage of industrial (and technological) development in a particular country. In the post-World War II period, Japan depended heavily upon operational technology from foreign sources, gradually replacing foreign engineering and design with indigenous scientific and technological capabilities to supplement foreign imports. "Unbundling" (and redesigning and repackaging) was a basic technique used by the Japanese in their industrial evolution.

A third misconception is that government-to-government aid programs can provide development of indigenous science and technology in universities and research laboratories which in turn can be channeled into the productive sectors. The fact is that rarely have the programs addressed themselves to the designing and engineering of "operational" technologies. One basic problem is that the lion's share of efforts go toward a long-term buildup of basic research ability, most of which is unrelated to the applied and development research that feeds into operational technologies.

A fourth myth is that industrial technology can be developed in university laboratories and industrial research institutes to help replace industrial systems traditionally supplied by foreign enterprise sources. The fact is that science and technology communities do not produce operational technology packages. Furthermore, even if they did, the linkages between these communities and the productive sectors are largely ineffective. Science and technology communities can perform an important ancillary role in support of industrial design and engineering efforts to improve, enhance, or supplement foreign enterprise sources of operational technology, but they cannot be the major supply source now or in the foreseeable future. Operational technologies will continue to be the products of enterprise units linked to technology generating units. The university community can best help by developing human resources to take a more positive role in creative design and engineering activities.

DILEMMAS OF MANAGING TECHNOLOGICAL DEVELOPMENT IN LATIN AMERICA

As Latin American governments have sought to intervene in the development process, they have inevitably infringed upon enterprise decisions governing production and marketing activities. In the technology field, administered guidelines and regulations have sought to lead (or compel) enterprises into new channels of supply (from indigenous sources to replace foreign suppliers) or to screen technology imports to eliminate restrictive clauses in foreign licenses, to assure that the price paid is not excessive, and to influence decisions in the choice of technology "appropriate" to the national endowment and development goals. The inevitable difficulties (and dilemmas) lie in the basic conflict between commercial interests to maximize profits in price-distorted economies and the achievement of national developmental goals, which, if adhered to, would often reduce realizable profits and, more importantly, would seriously complicate the life of enterprise managers. The fact is that "dependence" upon foreign technology is a form of risk aversion for the private enterprise, and the foreign patent and/or trademark provide positive reinforcement to the effective exploitation of protected domestic markets.

In response to the foregoing dilemma, Latin American governments have increasingly turned to administered controls to intervene in technology markets. This has subsequently given rise to another set of problems. One is that technology markets are highly complex in nature and the sheer quantum of what must be monitored poses monumental tasks for government bureaucracies. Moreover, efforts to screen and control acquired technology, or to impose various restrictions on what should be bought and the amounts that are paid, merely serve to reduce the supply of technology without offering commercially viable alternatives for technological development from within the economy.

Another dilemma concerns short-term gains versus long-term growth. National efforts to develop indigenous technological capabilities (to make decisions without persistent dependence upon foreign aid, to negotiate more effectively for technology components, to adapt acquired technology as needed, and to produce technology where appropriate), and to improve bargaining positions vis-a-vis foreign investors and other technology suppliers may result in production losses, at least in the short run. In the long run, however, a more dynamic and self-reliant technology structure that reaches into production systems can contribute significantly to productivity (more efficient and extensive utilization of available resources) as well as to the general level of employment and national output. Difficulties and frustration in national policy formulation are inevitable if government authorities fail to recognize the trade-offs in this area, but insist instead on having their cake and eating it too.

U.S. CORPORATE RESPONSE TO THE
CHANGING ENVIRONMENT

In response to this new set of national development objectives involving the technology component, a number of U.S.-based companies have been entering into technology transfer agreements that are significantly more responsive than in the past to the emerging demands for new modes and content in technology acquisitions by the newly industrializing nations, particularly in Latin America. The new generation of agreements (see below) reflects, in part, some of the profound changes that have occurred in the world economy, as well as changing perceptions of certain U.S. corporations as to how they may use their technology assets and know-how in new and more imaginative ways, and at the same time continue to earn a return on their corporate assets. These innovations in corporate involvements center around the technology component of industrial systems, but they also involve profound adjustments in international marketing and production strategies of involved companies.

From the corporate perspective, the attractions of equity investment in, and managerial control of, foreign facilities are waning.[4] A growing number of multinational corporations have now decided that the risks associated with overseas capital investments have become too high for realized rates of return. Aside from political uncertainties in a widening area of the world, there are the economic vicissitudes brought on by world inflation, exchange rate revaluations, and recessionary cycles, all of which have added to the risks of locking into fixed investments in a world of changing circumstances. These uncertainties have been compounded by the fragmentation of world markets resulting from import substitution behind tariff barriers and regional trading blocs as a partial offset to the inefficiencies of protected national economies. The growth of host country restrictions, regulations, and limitations on foreign investment has also tended to detract from this traditional mode of overseas involvement.

Another feature of the new technology-sharing agreements is the buy-back arrangement whereby the supplier agrees to accept partial payment in product. Once regarded as a necessary evil for market entry or retention of market share, these arrangements are coming to be viewed by U.S. corporations as a hedge against import restrictions and exchange controls remitted earnings. In some cases, companies find offshore manufacture of components and parts less costly than in the U.S. and, in those cases, have a double incentive to enter into buy-back arrangements.

Another factor which has contributed to the accommodating response by U.S. corporations has been the progressive advance in bargaining power that countries like Brazil and Mexico are now able to exert in negotiations with multinationals. This enhanced bargaining leverage is derived from a variety of new conditions, any one of which in and of itself, is not necessarily determining; but, combined, these new conditions result in a marked shift in the balance of bargaining power between technology suppliers and purchasers in favor of the latter. The shift in bargaining leverage is attributable in part to the proliferation of alternative sources of industrial technology from Japan and Western Europe.

The supportive interventionist role played by Latin American governments in the technology transfer process also has enhanced the bargaining positions of Latin American enterprises. Latin American governments have adopted a variety of other supportive roles, ranging from acting as prime negotiator and purchasing agent in technology transactions to the erection of government agencies to screen and control incoming technology and capital investments.

Both Mexico and Colombia have begun to use their oil and mineral resources as leverage in acquiring industrial facilities and know-how to process their resources for world markets.

Another factor which has contributed to the shift in bargaining leverage has been the perceptible upgrading in recent years of the knowledge and skills which technology purchasers in less developed countries (LDCs) bring to bear in negotiation sessions with multinational corporations. (See discussion of Negotiating for Technology Acquisitions, Chapter V.)

NEW GENERATION OF TECHNOLOGY-SHARING AGREEMENTS

The new generation of technology-sharing agreements is significantly more responsive than traditional licensing and investment modes to the emerging demands by newly industrializing nations for new types of and content in technology acquisitions. Under these new arrangements, the international competitiveness and self-generating capabilities of LDC enterprise personnel in the adaptive engineering process is an invaluable contribution to the self-reliance that LDC governments have been so anxiously seeking. Binding arrangements to export a percentage of production output assures that the LDC enterprise is meeting internationally competitive quality and performance standards, and (to the extent that export prices reflect costs) international cost competitiveness. An overview of the principal changes that have occurred in the marketing, production, and engineering fields follows.

Changes in the Marketing Function

With a view toward improving the productivity of resource utilization and balance-of-payments positions, many development authorities have called for moving national enterprises from the shelter of protected markets, characteristic of the import substitution phase of industrialization, into the more competitive environments of regional and world export markets. This has placed considerable demands upon technology suppliers to assist LDC enterprises in the logistics of international marketing and distribution. One significant innovation which U.S. corporations are making in this area is to permit purchaser enterprises in developing world countries to channel their products to world markets through their own highly developed and efficient international marketing systems. From the developing-nation viewpoint, this provides reassurance about the economic efficiency of installed plant and equipment.[5]

A second significant change which is taking place in the marketing function of the new technology-sharing agreements has been the granting of trademark rights by U.S. corporations to the purchaser enterprise. The benefits derived by the newly industrializing nations are both practical and psychological. By committing its trademark and logo, a U.S. firm is, in effect, guaranteeing that the final product will be as good in every respect as any product coming off its own production lines. This means that the technology purchaser can anticipate the transfer and constant updating of those production methods and product design modifications which comprise the U.S. firm's latest technology. This situation requires that the U.S. company spend an extraordinary amount of time training workers of the purchasing enterprise in production techniques so that the product can be interchangeable with that which is manufactured at the firm's other plants.

An important distinction needs to be drawn here between the

above-described situation and the practice among multinational corporations of fully exploiting internationally recognized trade names and logos in LDC markets. In the latter case, the product is typically manufactured in an owned and controlled operation of the multinational, located either in the home country or in an LDC. Such products frequently constitute overwhelming competition for locally designed and manufactured products, carrying unfamiliar trademarks. It is this situation which has prompted development authorities, particularly in Mexico, to require that goods produced under international licenses and carrying foreign trademarks also be marked with a local trade name and logo. For example, Union Carbide Mexicana, S.A. marks all of its products with the Union Carbide logo, coupled with the name and sign of "El Pilon" or the cat. In this way, it is hoped, the Mexican public will come to associate those products as much with a national company and national capabilities as with a foreign multinational.

A final innovational dimension in the marketing function encountered in some of the new agreements is the buy-back arrangement. Under buy-back arrangements, the technology supplier agrees to accept partial payment for the technology in product, rather than monetary compensation, which is then distributed to the supplier enterprise's worldwide customers or subsidiaries. The overriding value to an LDC enterprise of such an arrangement is the guaranteed level of exports. Such exports make the technology transfer a self-financing proposition; but, above and beyond being assured the means of paying for the technology transplant, the purchaser enterprise is guaranteed a hard currency buyer of its product.

Changes in the Production Function

The new technology-sharing agreements represent a radical departure from the traditional approach U.S. corporations have taken toward managing technological assets. In the past, it was only late in a product's life cycle—once the production techniques had become generally available—that the corporation was prepared to release technology. Today, however, as the case material reveals, a growing segment of U.S. industry is prepared to sell the most sophisticated and latest generation technology available, and its release is often under terms that assure rapid and efficient implantation of an internationally competitive production capability. Acquiring internationally competitive technology and production systems (high-volume, cost-efficient, and quality-controlled products) is particularly compelling to newly industrializing nations in that it permits the saving or earning of sorely-needed foreign exchange (through either import substitution and/or export promotion) with which to further expand and upgrade industrial production. Earning of hard currency is also critical in light of the debt burden now carried by these countries.

In addition to providing a scope and level of technology which permits quick entry into world markets, another innovation in the production function evident in the new agreements is the training component. Often such arrangements are accompanied by intensive educational and technical programs designed to create a self-sufficient manpower base within the country capable of managing and operating the newly acquired plants or production processes.

A final and extremely significant change taking place in the production area has been the ancillary function performed by U.S. supplier corporations in the progressive development of domestic capital goods industries and related supplier plants as contributions to overall industrial growth and development. The development of forward and backward linkages has been an integral part of several of the new agreements, laying the necessary base for self-sufficient production.

Changes in the RD&E Function

The contribution to indigenous design and engineering capabilities is another important innovational dimension emerging in the new agreements. These capabilities are viewed as essential skills needed to adapt foreign product designs and production techniques to indigenous factors of production and, more importantly, to generate their own technology. Training in design-engineering is often imparted through contracts calling for joint execution of plant engineering.

Joint research efforts between MNCs and LDC enterprises to develop new product designs or processes for eventual entry into world markets also represents a departure from the way R&D is traditionally carried out.

Another change in the way in which RD&E is carried out by the corporation and which is also extremely supportive of development objectives in the newly industrializing nations has been the structuring of enterprise relations so as to wean the LDC enterprise from foreign technology sources. Engendering technological self-reliance is a principal objective in the new contract relations being formulated in Mexico, Brazil, and Colombia.

NEED FOR NEW INSTITUTIONAL MECHANISMS

Currently, the issue of technology transfers between U.S. and Latin American enterprises is beset by critical problems associated with a growing Latin American demand for new technologies and the inadequate U.S.-firm supply response. The situation will not be alleviated at least in the near future. The underlying reasons for the inadequacy of U.S. enterprise response are: (a) the traditional sources of the bulk of U.S. industrial technology have been the larger-size firms in the Fortune 1000 list, and they are reluctant to share technology on other than an equity investment or related licensing arrangement; and (b) the medium to smaller size firms (with sales below $100 million a year) are not able to obtain financing for the outright sale of manufacturing know-how and related design-engineering services that are typically associated with industrial technology transfers. It is for this reason that the final chapter is devoted: (a) to analysis of individual country needs for new institutional mechanisms; and (b) to specific recommendations for new institutional mechanisms to bridge these gaps.

On the Latin American side, there is an implicit demand for a financial mechanism to cover the outright purchase of industrial know-how from U.S. enterprise sources. (See discussion of Technology Transfer Service Corporation in Chapter V.) For U.S. technical assistance that focuses upon benefiting the urban and rural poor and the promotion of small-scale enterprise to provide employment and income to the poverty sectors—and at the same time seeks to involve segments of U.S. industry in providing technology components to small-scale enterprise—recommendations are presented for a Small Enterprise Development Corporation to administer programs on a bilateral basis between the U.S. and any other interested Latin American country.

FOOTNOTES

[1]This is a lesson the more advanced Latin American governments have learned from the Japanese experience, where, beginning in the early 1950s, the Japanese Government screened all foreign investments and leasing agreements to minimize the adverse side-effects of preemptive foreign presence or restrictive licensing arrangements.

[2]The italicized terms may be defined as follows: *screening* includes the monitoring, evaluation and assessment of foreign technologies; *controlling* includes restrictions on the inflow of foreign technology based on appropriateness to national development goals; *planning* includes policy coordination and project formulation; *searching* includes both creation of an information system and individual search and evaluation activities; *negotiating* includes activities of the parties negotiating and the new government monitoring role; *training* includes all activities related to know-how transmission through people; *supporting* includes services such as standard setting, patent registration and extension services; *using,* the ultimate goal at which any technology transfer system is aimed, includes installation, operation, and maintenance; and *generating* includes research (basic and applied) and design and engineering of products and production systems (RD&E).

[3]For fuller discussion, see Jack Baranson, "The Cornucopian Politics of World Development," *The Bulletin of Atomic Scientists.* November 1978.

[4]The traditional viewpoint has been that the release of technology, particularly unique and proprietary technology, would weaken and ultimately erode a firm's competitiveness in world markets. A corollary to this belief was the conviction that a return on investment was earned only when a product was developed and successfully commercialized in the marketplace. Continued returns throughout the product's life cycle could be assured only by retaining the technology within the corporate family. It was only very late in a product's life cycle—once the production techniques had become generally available—that the corporation was prepared to release the technology, and then its release was through the traditional transfer modes of direct foreign investment and licensing of patents and trademarks.

[5]This point and several others that follow, are exemplified in the case materials contained in the country chapters.

CHAPTER II
BRAZIL*

INTRODUCTION

Among all Latin American countries, Brazil is in the forefront of recognizing the significance of the technology factor in national growth and development. There is an emerging consciousness of the role of foreign enterprises and their impact upon national technological development and a determination on the part of the government to intervene in the technology transfer channels for the national interest. The traditional modes of foreign investments in manufacturing facilities are being challenged in Brazil, and foreign firms are encountering considerable difficulties and dilemmas—including mounting restrictions on required imports, barriers to the expansion of manufacturing operations, and growing demands by governmental authorities to increase Brazilian exports of manufactured goods and to share sophisticated (internationally competitive) technology with Brazilian enterprise.

The reasons for these changes are articulated in national development objectives, which are aimed at expanding Brazilian-owned and controlled enterprise and the technological self-reliance of the economy at large. These objectives are viewed as an important contribution to the dynamics of economic growth in Brazil. The progressive development of a domestic capital goods industry, with ancillary design and engineering capabilities, is regarded as another vital ingredient of growth dynamics and the drive toward technological self-sufficiency.

The Brazilian experience dramatizes the need for a reorientation upon the part of U.S. enterprise toward its business involvement in newly industrializing countries. The days of majority-owned and management-controlled investments inevitably are giving way to minority interest involvement in the Brazilian economy. What is happening in Brazil is an extension of what has already occurred in Japan, Eastern Europe and other state-managed economies. This trend in Brazil need not mean the progressive exclusion of U.S. enterprise; on the contrary, it raises new opportunities for U.S. firms to participate through the sale of equipment, technical and management services, and component and materials interchange.

---

*A list of abbreviations will be found at the end of the Chapter.

The case material in this chapter concerns high technology industries such as aircraft, computers, and the design and engineering of
petrochemical plants. In each of these areas, the Brazilian Government
is pursuing policies aimed at precluding foreign enterprise considered to
constitute overpowering competition to the emerging Brazilian industry. At the same time, Brazil is anxious to have U.S. enterprise participation in the Brazilian economy as minority shareholders, yielding the
management of industrial facilities to Brazilian control. The U.S. firm is
being sought as a supplier of essential technology and, whenever possible, one that will facilitate access to world markets where Brazilian
firms can earn much-needed foreign exchange.

In both the aircraft and computer industries, Brazilian enterprise
groups, after many difficulties, have succeeded in negotiating management service contracts with U.S. firms for manufacturing technology.
In the petrochemical field, a variety of joint ventures are being negotiated with U.S. and other foreign firms, taking minority share positions
under Brazilian managerial control.

THE ECONOMY AND TECHNOLOGY

Economic Trends

From 1967 to 1973 Brazil witnessed a period of remarkable economic growth, with GDP rising at a real rate of approximately eleven
percent per year and industrial value-added rising by thirteen percent
per annum. During this period, several of the country's sources of rapid
economic growth were directly or indirectly related to its technology
transfer policy. These sources of development included: (a) a rapid
growth of public sector investments; (b) an inflow of foreign capital
and technology; (c) a twenty-five percent per year annual growth of
manufactured exports; and (d) a broad policy of import substitution
(aimed at the development of reasonably efficient basic industries and
capital equipment industries that contribute to indigenous engineering
efforts).

The 1973-1974 oil crisis proved to be a turning point in the development of the Brazilian economy. Brazil's overwhelming dependence
on imported petroleum (over fifty percent) has since contributed to the
country's two most significant economic problems—accelerating inflation and a deteriorating balance-of-payment situation which has also
been affected by increases in agricultural imports due to crop failures
and continued imports of capital goods and machinery. Inflation has
remained a problem due to the continued high growth of demand in the
face of constricted imports and increased protection of domestic industry.

Given its recurring difficulties with inflation and external debt, the Brazilian Government has established four major economic goals, all of which are being addressed through attempts to increase the country's technological capabilities. Advanced agricultural technology contributes to an achievement of the goal of an accelerated growth of the agriculture sector. To realize the goal of a reduced dependency on imported petroleum, foreign and indigenous technology is being used to develop the nation's vast hydroelectric potential, to initiate nuclear power production, to substitute alcohol for gasoline and to introduce energy conservation measures. In order to maintain its expansion of manufactured exports, Brazil must further develop its technological base in order to remain internationally competitive. Finally, in pursuit of the goal of continued import substitution, the Brazilian government has looked to technological development as a solution, especially in the capital goods and machine building industry.

Technology Component in National Development Objectives

The "technology component" looms large in Brazil's national development objectives. It is considered a vital ingredient of dynamic economic growth and industrial competitiveness in world markets. To Brazilian Government officials responsible for economic growth and national development, the "technology component" has come to mean the development of indigenous capabilities to adapt or redesign product and component designs and related manufacturing methods acquired from foreign sources, or, if necessary, to design and engineer products and processes to the needs and conditions of the Brazilian economy. An integral part of national technological development policies is to intervene in technology flows from foreign sources with a view toward limiting foreign investments and industrial licensing arrangements that would inhibit or be harmful to the growth and development of indigenous design and engineering capabilities and supporting infrastructures (such as capital goods industries that contribute to domestic design and engineering efforts). The Brazilian Government has also provided public funds to foster domestic design and engineering activities.

Comprehensive plans for achieving these goals and objectives are embodied in a National Development Plan which is revised annually and which details the systematic and sustained efforts needed to control and direct desired change. Recent plans have emphasized consolidation of the country into a modern market economy that is integrated into the international economy. The tactical means toward that end involves the use of strong business structures, created through a policy of mergers, financial conglomerates and mixed industrial-financial companies; the development of indigenous capabilities to absorb external savings, technology, and managerial talent; the use of modern industrial technology as a means of gaining competitive strength in a large number of industrial and infrastructural sectors; and the adoption of a clear and consistent policy with regard to multinational corporations and foreign capital in general.

Long-range national development objectives in Brazil call for expanding nationally-owned and controlled enterprises and the technological self-reliance of the economy at large. These objectives are viewed as an important contribution to the dynamics of economic growth in Brazil. The progressive development of a domestic capital goods industry, with ancillary design and engineering capabilities, is regarded as another vital ingredient of growth dynamics and the drive toward technological self-sufficiency. Brazilian authorities have been acutely aware for some time that traditional modes of foreign investments in manufacturing facilities are not supportive of, and in some cases, are counterproductive to the attainment of economic and technological development goals. As a result, U.S. firms seeking a share of the attractive Brazilian market have met with numerous challenges and difficulties posed by government authorities. Foremost among these have been mounting restrictions on required imports, barriers to the expansion of manufacturing operations, and growing demand by governmental authorities to increase Brazilian exports of manufactured goods and to share sophisticated (internationally competitive) technology with Brazilian enterprise.

Particularly in high technology industries, such as aircraft, computers, and the design and engineering of petrochemical plants, the Brazilian Government is pursuing policies aimed at precluding foreign enterprise considered to constitute overpowering competition to the emerging Brazilian industry. At the same time, Brazil is anxious to have U.S. enterprise participation in the Brazilian economy as minority shareholders, yielding the management of industrial facilities to Brazilian control. The U.S. firm is being sought as a supplier of essential technology and, whenever possible, one that will facilitate access to world markets where Brazilian firms can earn much-needed foreign exchange.

An example of the new role being assigned to foreign enterprise in Brazil's economy is the tripartite shareholding model. Devised by the state-owned petrochemical company, PETROQUISA, the model calls for participation of the government, of national private capital and of foreign capital in near equal proportions at the petrochemical complex in Bahia, a rapidly growing petrochemical center in the northeast. The participation of national private capital falls in most cases to national entrepreneurs whose traditional fields of activity are other than petrochemicals. Fiscal incentives and the protection and safety offered by the presence of a "strong partner"—PETROQUISA—are the major incentives inducing Brazilian entrepreneurs into this field. The government recognizes that without its intervention in this manner, the industry would continue to be dominated by foreign corporations.

In order for Brazil to fully implement its national development objective of expanded technological autonomy, it must continue to develop its technical manpower capabilities. In spite of substantial cadres of university-trained scientists and engineers and adequate capabilities in standard technologies, shortages still prevail in experienced managers, engineers, and technicians required for the broad spectrum of new industrial endeavors the economy is now attempting to get underway. Nor is there in place an institutional capability at the enterprise level which can conduct the intricate D/E needed to develop these industries. Consulting engineering firms engaged in the adaptive design and engineering of plants, processes and equipment are limited in number, and RD&E facilities at the enterprise level are rare.

TECHNOLOGY SUPPORT STRUCTURES AND MECHANISMS

Government

The Brazilian Government has used a broad variety of mechanisms to implement its technological development objectives. First, realizing the importance of the productive sectors in advancing technological growth, the government is providing direct financial assistance to technology users for the selection, research and development of product and process technology. Secondly, government agencies provide direct technical assistance to the firm through technical, consulting and engineering services. Third, the government is expanding its role as a source and disseminator of scientific and technological information. Fourth, certain government ministries are formulating their own research and development programs. Other government funding is applied to building up the indigenous industrial infrastructure, through strengthening the financial structure of the firm, reinforcing the demand for technology, augmenting the legal-regulatory environment to control the influx of technology, and broadening the skilled manpower base through the growth of diverse training programs.

In designing implementation mechanisms, Brazilian authorities have drawn a fundamental distinction between importation of "ready-made" technology and the effective transfer of technology. The latter is viewed in Brazilian policy as a process involving several steps: (a) knowledge of what technology is needed; (b) knowledge of how to negotiate for it on advantageous terms; (c) the capability to adapt and absorb newly acquired production systems; and (d) the ability to reproduce or create technology in selective areas.

Certain bureaucratic organizations have been revitalized through new capabilities and the assignment of new responsibilities, such as a vastly expanded and strengthened tax collection authority. The educational system has similarly been enlarged and reoriented toward production of trained manpower. For example, in addition to the SENAI program (National Service for Industrial Apprenticeship), formed in 1942 and supported by a one percent payroll levy on all industries, there is the National Program for Executive Training (PNTE), aimed at improving and upgrading management capabilities among the national enterprises, public and private.

Entirely new organizations have been created with important new powers, such as the Industrial Development Council (CDI) which grants government fiscal incentives for eligible investment projects. National financial institutions have developed innovative ways to facilitate the accumulation of investment capital and have mobilized the funds into priority growth sectors, such as automotive, chemical, and iron and steel. The growth and diversification of exports have been fostered through a highly successful set of tax incentives, developed by the government.

Among Brazilian Government efforts toward maximum resource utilization, perhaps the most dramatic has been its direct control of the economy through the creation of large state-owned enterprises. Since 1964, there has been a vast proliferation and expansion of government-run companies, based on the assumption that most national private firms as yet lack the financial, managerial, and technical resources for large undertakings.

The state runs or has a share in some of Brazil's largest enterprises, including: the country's largest steel producer, Companhia Siderurgica Nacional; its largest iron ore producer, the Companhia Vale do Rio Doce; the oil monopoly, PETROBRAS; the electricity generating monopoly, ELECTROBRAS; the telecommunications group, TELE-BRAS; and the aircraft manufacturer, EMBRARER. Two unprofitable businesses are also owned by the government: the shipping concern, Loide Brasileiro, and the nationalized railways, Rede Ferroviaria Federal. In 1970 a detailed study by *Visao*, a Brazilian magazine similar to *Business Week*, indicated that sixteen of Brazil's twenty largest firms were operated by the state, which owned eighty-six percent of the total assets involved.

The state also has assumed a pivotal role in Brazil's capital markets. Some sixty percent of all investment during the growth period 1967 to 1973 was undertaken by the government. Since inflation has been on the increase, Brazilians save through the state's institutions, because the private sector cannot provide the guarantees (through price indexing, for example) that savers have come to expect. The state-run Banco do Brasil has almost one quarter of all bank deposits, and the government itself owns fifteen commercial and eleven development banks.

Development of National Enterprises

An essential element of Brazilian Government policy has been the creation of an appropriate balance between national and foreign enterprise. Implicit in this desired objective has been the need for government intervention in national enterprise development, given the powerful and pervasive involvement of foreign investment in the Brazilian economy.[1] This intervention has taken form in a variety of industrial and economic development measures designed to strengthen the financial, organizational, and commercial viability of the Brazilian enterprise.

To strengthen the financial structure of national firms, the government has provided support to projects of large national enterprises or to the participation of national enterprises in large-scale undertakings in basic sectors and/or leading technology. This support has been carried out through several programs of the National Development Bank (BNDE), PETROBRAS' petrochemical subsidiary (PETROQUISA), and other governmental finance organizations. In this area of activity are financial and fiscal support to assist Brazilian firms in associating themselves in joint venture projects which may go so far as providing the Brazilian partner sufficient capital to permit its share in the undertaking.

In addition to direct and equity financing, the government has sought to strengthen demand, both foreign and domestic, for Brazilian manufactured goods. To raise the level of quality and technological sophistication of production, and thereby enhance competitiveness, new mechanisms have been created to establish and monitor industrial norms and standards. The national industrial structure has also been modernized and strengthened through improvements in the legal and regulatory environment. An important new element in this environment is the National Institute for Industrial Property (INPI) which has established guidelines for national enterprises in negotiating with foreign firms for technology.

Government Planning

The agency which is primarily responsible for overall planning and coordination of Brazilian science and technology policy is the Planning Secretariat (SEPLAN). Its main functions are: (a) to formulate a global science and technology policy; (b) to ensure effective implementation of the PBDCT; (c) to ensure compatibility among S&T policies at the federal, state and municipal levels; and (d) to guide other government agencies which have responsibility for science and technology development. The National Council for Scientific Technological Development (CNPq), subordinate to SEPLAN, has considerable responsiblity in planning S&T policy. Its main activities are: (a) to assist in the preparation of the PBDCT; (b) to promote a national system for the collection, analysis and dissemination of information on S&T development; (c) to improve human resources by providing training programs; and (d) to promote linkages between public and private sectors.[2]

The Ministry of Industry and Commerce is the agency which has major responsiblity for industrial development. MIC now has an Industrial Technology Secretariat (STI) which: (a) regulates industrial patents, technology transfer and metrology; (b) provides direct financial support for specific technologies in priority sectors; (c) offers technical and information services to private firms; and (d) sponsors direct government research and development programs. STI is the first sectoral science/technology entity to be established within a ministry; similar entities are projected for other agencies.

STI coordinates three important subordinate agencies—the National Technology Institute (INT), the (previously mentioned) National Institute for Industrial Property (INPI), and the National Institute of Metrology, Normalization and Industrial Quality (INMETRO). INT is responsible for the R&D elements of STI. INPI is charged with registering patents and trademarks and approving licensing and technical assistance agreements. INMETRO, still in the organizational stage, is aiming to maintain high industrial standards through a national system of quality control regulations.

INPI is especially important in formulating Brazilian S&T policy. It is the agency which screens and regulates technology agreements in accordance with Ordinance 15 ("Normative Act"), which was promulgated by the president of INPI on September 11, 1975, under authority of the Industrial Property Code Laws. (See Appendix for synopsis of Ordinance 15.) It attempts to spell out a comprehensive set of rules and regulations controlling the flow of technology into and out of Brazil. INPI guidelines are: (a) to favor the importation of technology over the importation of capital goods; (b) to acquire technology instead of "renting" it; (c) to eliminate contractual or implicit restrictions on local absorption and dissemination of technology; and (d) to discourage approval of patented contracts.

The INPI has been criticized by some U.S. firms doing business in Brazil as following a purposeful policy of "benign neglect" in issuing patents to foreign holders. They complain about long delays, inefficient handling of applications and staff shortages which contribute to slow processing of technology applications. Technology applications are often delayed as much as one year, while patent applications take over two years to be processed. Further, the regulations of Ordinance 15 place harsh conditions on foreign companies, thus reducing the number of applications which actually survive the screening process.

The Council of Industrial Development (CDI), under the MIC, is the government agency which determines the eligibility of new investment proposals for a wide range of fiscal incentives offered by the Brazilian Government, such as exemptions from taxes and import duties, accelerated depreciation of capital, and financing from government sources. CDI has played a significant role in setting Brazilian industrial policy. The choice of technology is not as important to CDI as is the viability of an investment plan, and the investor's ability to carry it out. CDI does, nevertheless, determine whether the proposed technology is suitable for regional or sectoral development. INPI works closely with CDI on questions of technology transfer. INPI representatives sit in on CDI "sectoral groups," and entrepreneurs who receive the CDI certificate must agree to follow INPI standards.

In the face of limited energy supplies and balance-of-payments problems, the CDI has become much more stringent in granting incentives to entrepreneurs and in approving projects. Industrial and capital goods, basic metal-producing industries and chemicals and petrochemicals are top priority projects. CDI now favors complete investment programs over isolated importation of machinery, and encourages foreign investors to import two-thirds of their equipment without foreign exchange coverage. These recent policy changes have made it more difficult for the investor to apply for government incentives.

Two other government regulatory agencies control technology transfer. The Department of Supervision and Registration of Foreign Capital (FIRCE) works in conjunction with INPI to control payments for royalties, licenses and technical assistance in compliance with Ordinance 15. The Foreign Commerce Board (CACEX), a department of the Bank of Brazil, is charged with controlling all export/import transactions. It is CACEX which supervises the prices of all imports and determines whether a given import has a Brazilian equivalent (there are no tax benefits if there is an equivalent).

Unlike other Latin American countries, individual Brazilian state agencies have considerable autonomy and flexibility in organizing for science and technology. State agencies are most active in infrastructural development and in projects which are aimed at fostering the growth of private domestic enterprises. The state of Sao Paulo has been especially active in developing Brazilian capabilities in these areas; several of its agencies will be mentioned to illustrate types of state activities. The Secretariat of Culture, Science and Technology (SCCT) is the Sao Paulo agency charged with setting science and technology policy at the state level. Since its inception in 1975, the SCCT has been active in transforming many state research institutes into public companies, and in establishing the Sao Paulo governmental network for science and technology. The subsequently dissolved State Council of Technology (CET) previously served functions similar to the SCCT.

The Sao Paulo Program for Science and Technology (PROCET), originally created by CET, is developing a state system to reorganize and strengthen state research institutions, and to reinforce their linkages with specific segments of the private sector. Further, PROCET is seeking to develop the technical competence necessary to plan and coordinate science and technology activities. PROCET was originally financed with a U.S. AID $15 million loan, with matching funds from the Sao Paulo Government.

The Financial Community

The primary institutions identified in the financial community are government agencies. The Central Bank of Brazil, in the Ministry of Finance, controls transactions relating to payments for royalties and fees abroad. The Bank of Brazil is state-owned and is the largest commercial bank in the country.

The Agency for the Financing of Studies and Projects (FINEP), subordinate to SEPLAN, is a public company which: (a) has responsibility for overall S&T planning; (b) gives direct financial support for specific technologies and technical assistance in the private sector; (c) administers the National Fund for S&T development; and (d) conducts technical training programs.

Closely related to SEPLAN is the National Economic Development Bank, a public company which has significantly contributed to economic development in Brazil through direct support of the private industrial sector. Its objectives are to: (a) stimulate exports; (b) support regional and state development banks; (c) fund technical development projects; and (d) strengthen small-to-medium-sized companies.

BNDE has several subsidiaries that finance national and international sales of Brazilian equipment, provide capital participation in various sectors, and supply capital for private Brazilian companies and work through other investment banks to subsidize certain projects. Through FUNTEC (Development Fund for Science and Technology), BNDE provides non-reimbursable monies for research at the university and enterprise level. Through other associated organizations, they support large industrial organizations and finance mergers and reorganization aimed at strengthening national companies.

At the state level, the Sao Paulo Fund for Scientific and Technology Development (FUNCET) finances specific technological development projects within industry and/or research institutes. FUNCET projects have emphasized augmenting the technical capabilities within the private sector, and the agency has funded a combination of quality control and research and development projects.

The Development Bank of the State of Sao Paulo (BADESP) is a corporation in which the state has majority interest. BADESP is the implementing agency for certain federal technological development programs. Through its various departments, BADESP provides direct loans to many types of enterprises to upgrade their technology.

One criticism of BADESP has been its emphasis in project evaluation upon the commercial segment to the exclusion of technical considerations. Another criticism of BADESP funding has been its possible overcommitment to subsidized industrial R&D as a substitute for imported technology. Funds of this kind are particularly effective where the emphasis is upon technology loans to commercial organizations which may then use borrowed funds to contract for local design and engineering of technology.

The Science and Technology Community

A group of some importance in Brazil's research and development network is the National Institute of Technology (INT). At present, INT conducts research and development work on a contract basis for individual industries, institutes, and universities. INT also undertakes special priority projects for STI. Almost all government ministries are involved in R&D activities, especially Mines and Energy, Agriculture, Transportation and Communications.

At the enterprise level, many state and private firms finance their own research institutes. CTA has created a research and development institute to study aerospace technology. CENPAS, part of PETRO-QUISA, conducts research on petroleum-related technology, emphasizing the design and engineering function. CEPED is a research entity which reports to the State of Bahia. In addition, many other firms have in-house R&D capacity which is often partially or wholly supported by the Brazilian Government. For example, Promon Engenharia, S.A., a large private firm, has recently created CTP, which does R&D on products and processes directly related to commercial development.

Individual Brazilian states are especially active in sponsoring research institutes. The Technology Research Institute of Sao Paulo (IPT) conducts research on industrial engineering problems encountered in the public and private sectors. The Bahia Research Institute (CEPED), the Institute of Technology of the State of Pernambuco (ITEP), and the Minas Gerais Technological Center (CETEC) are other state entities which undertake research and development projects.

An innovative facility is the Institute of Industrial Development (INDI) in the State of Minas Gerais, part of the Ministry of Industry, Commerce and Tourism, which does project promotion work based on market surveys and feasibility studies it carries out. One of the most significant thrusts of INDI activity is its mediation in negotiating joint ventures between foreign and Brazilian companies, specifically in the cellulose, cement, automotive and fertilizer industries.

Despite the proliferation of government-sponsored R&D facilities in universities, and other research institutes, these facilities rarely have effective linkages with productive activities. According to one survey,[3] the vast majority of research institutes have no linkage with industry. In order to bridge this gap, more programs are needed which will assist large, medium, and small firms in commercializing technological innovation.

Business Enterprise

In the following section, we shall focus on the Brazilian enterprise community—both the public and private sector. In addition to identifying the participants in this community, we have analyzed some of the problems this community encounters in achieving technological self-sufficiency in its interactions with foreign and domestic sources of technology and/or the Brazilian Government. Figure II-1 provides an assessment of functional capabilities of the enterprise community.

Public Sector

As in many LDCs, state-controlled enterprises in basic industries are becoming increasingly prevalent in Brazil. Since 1969, over 200 such companies have emerged, in which the government holds either partial or total equity. Total spending in the public sector was just under twenty-eight percent of GNP in 1973. Some of the leading state enterprises are: PETROBRAS (petroleum), SIDERBRAS (iron and steel), PETROQUISA (petrochemicals), COBRA (computers), EMBRAER (aircraft), ELETROBRAS (electricity), and NUCLEBRAS (nuclear energy).

State enterprises have been reasonably effective in planning, searching and negotiating for advanced technologies (see sections on aircraft, computers, and petrochemicals). Typically, ownership is shared with one major foreign partner, which serves as the principal source of technology. In negotiating technology agreements, the Brazilians insist that the foreign MNC take responsibility for instilling in Brazilians the technological capabilities necessary to take over operations. In the past, one criticism of the state enterprises has been that they have shown a risk-averting technological conservatism, demonstrated by an over-reliance on foreign technology sources and a minimal commitment to indigenous development of technology.

Smaller, privately owned firms claim that government agencies have an unfair advantage in dealing with government regulatory agencies. One study indicates that three-fourths of all technology contracts approved involve state enterprises.[4] Further, state enterprises are often the recipient of government fiscal incentives such as income tax exemptions and credits, exemption from customs duties, accelerated depreciation, rebate of indirect taxes and state and municipal tax holidays. In the aircraft and computer industries, for example, import duties on capital equipment are eliminated.

Private Sector

Large Brazilian firms have reached the state of development where they are rapidly acquiring the capabilities necessary to mobilize for the acquisition, adaptation and absorption of their own required technologies. Large firms are of three major types: (a) wholly-owned Brazilian MNCs; (b) firms with majority Brazilian ownership in a joint venture with a foreign affiliate; and (c) supplier companies which produce component parts for state enterprises such as EMBRAER or large automotive plants (see Figure II-1 for summary evaluation of enterprise capabilities).

FIGURE II-1. EVALUATION OF

MOBILIZING TECHNOLOGY

PUBLIC SECTOR

	BRAZILIAN MNC	U.S. BRAZILIAN (Majority) JOINT VENTURE	SUPPLIER INDUSTRIES (Aircraft-Automotive)	MEDIUM-SMALL ENTERPRISE
PLANNING	Adequate capabilities to plan mobilization and acquisition of technology requirements.	Varying degrees of dependence on U.S. affiliate and Brazilian government agencies.	Rely heavily upon purchaser enterprise groups (EMBRAER in aircraft and foreign automotive assemblers) subject to local content, import-export regulation.	Planning of technical adjustment limited to narrow range of choices and alternatives.
GENERATING	Most firms have in-house design-engineering capabilities. Rely in part on government labs and outside consulting design-engineering firms.	Generally rely upon U.S. partner for product-process design and engineering–varying degrees of technological evolution.	Almost entirely dependent upon component-parts purchaser enterprises for product-process-equipment design and engineering.	Limited range of capabilities to alter or generate technology–rely largely on technical competence of manager-owner.
SEARCHING	Adequate capabilities. Rely on foreign business and financial linkages for additional contacts.	Many Brazilian firms now in process of diversifying technology supply sources.	(Same as above.)	Contacts limited to equipment and materials suppliers, licensors, visits to industrial fairs.
NEGOTIATING	Adequate capabilities including financial resources to engage technical-legal support.	Negotiating position reinforced by Brazilian industrial property laws (INPI).	Dependent position (except large, diversified Brazilian enterprise).	Limited resources and capabilities to negotiate technology acquisition terms.
SUPPORTING	Rely on technical research labs and consulting firms for certain requirements.	Mixed reliance on foreign affiliates and outside Brazilian technical support services (materials testing and standards, local equipment suppliers.)	Most technical support services (including standards, quality control procedures) derived from purchaser enterprises.	Limited resources and low profile for risk taking to engage in technological experimentation.
TRAINING	Generally have in-house training or able to arrange for additional requirements with international licensing partners.	Mixed reliance on foreign affiliate, in-house, and outside support services.	Rely heavily on purchaser industry or outside-plant training groups.	Effort limited largely to on-job training of operator skills, some quality control procedures.
USING	Have in-house capabilities or able to arrange for under licensing and other contractual arrangements.	Adequate capabilities in part derived from foreign enterprise partners.	Procedures derived from equipment-materials suppliers, licensors, or component purchaser firms.	Technology-using capabilities relatively static and limited in product-process range.

ENTERPRISE CAPABILITIES IN
COMPONENTS (BRAZIL)

PRIVATE SECTOR

EMBRAER/CTA (Aircraft)	PETROBRAS (Oil)	COBRA/DIGIBRAS (Computers)	PETROQUISA (Petrochemicals)
Strong capabilities in identifying needs and formulating program to fulfill these needs. Planning is well managed.	Experienced in planning development of oil exploration, refining operations, and basic petrochemical industries.	As yet inexperienced in translating policy into projects. Coordination of activities weak.	Evidence of strong capability, particularly in coordinating basic and downstream industries planning.
Research and Development Institute, created by CTA, provides direct support to various independent companies. Northrop rates institute as comparable to private sector R&D facilities and among the most cost-effective R&D programs in operation. Does adaptation.	CENPES is research arm of PETROBRAS – which sometimes assign personnel to work on R&D projects. Competent, pragmatic approach to process engineering in standard range. Adept at dis-aggregating technology sophisticated adaptations and assignments for local design and manufacture of equipment.	Development work sponsored thus far through universities has been unsuccessful. Prototypes not able to be commercialized.	R&D arm is CEPED, with staff of 450. Original objective was lab research; trying to do more engineering and applied R&D. Gap still exists between lab and commercial technology development. Put technology in public domain.
In general, accurate assessment of their own needs has led to effective searches. Extensive knowledge of a variety of technology sources.	Substantial network to identify technology suppliers and for evaluating alternative technology sources.	Learning quickly but experience with Ferranti disappointing.	Aversion to risk-taking results in preference for proven, foreign technology. Unresolved conflict in search between immediate operative capability and the implantation of process design and engineering capabilities.
EMBRAER has demonstrated astute negotiating skills in acquiring the quantum and generation of technology it determines necessary. Also effective in getting support and training from supplier.	Experienced and well qualified technical, legal, financial staffs to evaluate and negotiate contracts.	Developing skillful negotiating techniques. Acquiring a clearer idea of what they want and how to get it.	Bargaining leverage strengthened by INPI regulations, but unofficial concessions must be made to MNC for some kinds of know-how. Able to obtain more favorable terms with Japanese than with U.S. firms.
A relatively new Institute for Standards and Measures has been organized to increase level of quality control and standardization throughout manufacturing cycle (suppliers, subcontractors, main contractors). Implementation is progressing.	In-house capabilities to maintain technical standards and quality control systems in plant operations.	Largely dependent on foreign company and/or consultants.	Limited resources and capabilities in this area, but CEPED has done some "revamping" of plants to achieve greater efficiencies or increased output.
Technical Educational Institute, established in 1950, has done exceptional work in preparing engineers in the fields of aeronautics and electronics.	Extensive in-house programs to train technical and managerial personnel.	Dependent on technology supplier.	Largely dependent on foreign technology source for training.
Effective in using technology although manufacturing costs are still too high to achieve international competitiveness.	Some criticism of economics of certain operations, but substantial technical capabilities to maintain and operate petrochemical plant facilities.	Considerable difficulty in utilizing operative technology at the enterprise level. Capability may improve with SYCOR.	Tendency to acquire most recent generation available hinders proficient use of know-how. Limited absorption inhibits adaptive capabilities.

Recent studies indicate that large Brazilian firms are still highly dependent on foreign sources of capital equipment and intermediate goods, in spite of the large percentage of end-products which are being produced domestically. The Brazilian Government's ongoing efforts to curb imports and encourage indigenous manufacturing of capital equipment and intermediate goods are likely to decrease continued dependence on foreign technologies.

Most large firms have not yet developed sophisticated in-house R&D capacity. These enterprises claim that foreign firms have generally been unwilling to transfer R&D activities to Brazil, nor has the Brazilian Government provided sufficient incentives to firms for the local establishment of R&D facilities. An example of one large firm which has developed its own R&D arm is Promon Engenharia, an architecture and engineering consulting firm. It has established the Promon Technology Center (CTP), which develops its own project ideas, attempts to solve technological problems, and organizes R&D training programs. The success of CTP may encourage other larger firms to create similar research centers.

Small-to-Medium-Sized Firms

Small-to-medium-sized enterprises, largely Brazilian owned and controlled, represent a significant and vital portion of the Brazilian private sector. These firms have limited capabilities in planning, searching and negotiating for new technologies, because of their weak bargaining position and rudimentary level of technical know-how.

They claim that larger firms are sufficiently organized to take advantage of government incentives, whereas smaller firms do not have the organizational capability to benefit from such assistance. As a result, smaller enterprises often lack the financial resources necessary to initiate new programs and upgrade technical capabilities. Smaller firms feel that the government has not adequately provided programs which take into account their special needs.

The limited productive capacity of smaller firms has contributed to rising importation of capital equipment and heavy dependence on foreign capital and ideas. Firms claim that the government has not adequately attempted to protect them from the high costs of these imports. One policy option recommended by the firms themselves is to strengthen the linkages between research institutes and the productive sector. Further, many smaller firms express the need for government-sponsored training programs for the mid-level technicians which will be needed to bring about relative technological autonomy in smaller enterprises.

Comparison and Overview

In assessing technology mobilization and transfer capabilities in Brazil's private and public sectors, several observations can be made. Figure II-1 provides an overview of their comparative assessments.

Planning and Generating. State enterprises such as PETROBRAS, PETROQUISA, EMBRAER and some of the larger private firms are able to plan overall technology acquisition requirements and even generate certain required segments. These larger enterprises generally have in-house RD&E facilities and have acquired the technical capabilities necessary to support newly created technologies. At the same time, however, there is continued dependence on foreign assistance in fulfilling these functions. Figure II-1 underlines the extensive role that foreign firms are playing in the technological development of Brazilian industry.

Small-to-medium-sized firms generally are not capable of devising plans for technology mobilization and of generating and supporting new technologies. These firms rely heavily on equipment and materials suppliers[5] for technological advancement. A recent IPEA study[5] indicates that innovation in these firms is less likely to come from within the firm than from an outside impetus such as higher fuel costs, innovation in a related industry, or response to increased demand for the firm's product.

Searching and Negotiating. In searching and negotiating for new technologies, state enterprises have often shown considerable adroitness in negotiating with foreign technology suppliers. However, the propensity for risk-aversion among these firms has limited their readiness to purchase "unbundled" elements of a given technology. While large firms are gradually acquiring searching and negotiating skills, there is still heavy reliance on foreign technical expertise. Small-to-medium-sized firms are inclined to rely on materials and equipment suppliers, without attempting to design or significantly adapt acquired technology.

Training and Support Functions. The management and technical training function is fulfilled in various ways depending on the type of enterprise. State and private firms, often connected with international technology suppliers, may do in-house training through Brazilian or foreign technicians or send personnel abroad to learn new skills. Small-to-medium-sized firms do predominantly on-the-job training, lacking sufficient financial or human capital to utilize more sophisticated methods.

Using Technology. Indigenous adaptation and management of new technologies without foreign technical assistance signifies an advanced stage of technological growth. Few Brazilian firms have reached this level, but certain state enterprises and large private firms are beginning to gain some control. Small-to-medium-sized firms, however, continue to be relatively static with limited adaptive capabilities. It should be noted that the Second National Plan for Scientific and Technological Development (II PBDCT) gives some indication of an awareness by the Brazilian Government of the shortcomings in the technological development of both public and private enterprises.

CASE STUDIES – U.S.-BRAZIL
ENTERPRISE RELATIONS

In both the aircraft and computer industries, Brazilian enterprise groups, after many difficulties, have succeeded in negotiating management services contracts with U.S. firms for manufacturing technology. In the petrochemical field, a variety of joint ventures is being negotiated, under the tripartite model, with U.S. and other foreign firms taking minority share positions under Brazilian managerial control. In all three of these sectors, as the case studies which follow illustrate, government financing and initiatives have played a predominant role.

Piper's Industrial Cooperation
Agreement with EMBRAER

Intent upon developing an indigenous, integrated aircraft industry— including airframes and engines—the Brazilian Government in 1974 put, in effect, an ultimatum to the country's major suppliers of general aviation aircraft. Continued participation in the Brazilian market, which, at that time, represented the single largest export market for U.S. light aircraft (general aviation) manufacturers, was made contingent upon a firm's willingness to take on a Brazilian partner and begin a light aircraft production program in Brazil. The domestic production program, it was understood, would enjoy all the government support and protection it needed, including the establishment of prohibitive tariffs on import competition. This decision by the government was based upon a sharp awareness of the financial as well as economic and technical benefits which the country forfeited if it continued to rely upon foreign manufacturers. The potential savings in foreign exchange reserves alone were compelling, in that approximately five percent of the country's total expenditures on imports in 1973 went to the U.S. aerospace industry, and the figure was even higher in 1974.

In spite of the fact that Cessna held more than sixty percent of the Brazilian market and enjoyed, as a result, a slightly more favored negotiating position, it was Piper that was prepared to accommodate the new set of conditions demanded by the Brazilian Government for continued involvement in the market. In midsummer 1974, Piper entered into a wide-ranging industrial cooperation program with Empresa Brasileira de Aeronautica, S.A. (EMBRAER), the state-owned aviation development and production firm. The program is actually based upon two separate agreements—one for single engine aircraft and the other for twin engine aircraft—which permit EMBRAER to select any Piper model it wishes for local production. Toward the end of their five-year agreement (1975), EMBRAER had already undertaken assembly work on Piper's popular Pathfinder, Cherokee, Cherokee Six, Lance, Seneca II, and Navajo, and Piper had shipped over 1,000 kits to Brazil.

Piper is responsible for providing the necessary assembly and parts manufacturing know-how, as well as for assisting in such areas as quality control, materials handling, and manufacturing. Piper has an option to use its international distribution system for aircraft that may be exported from Brazil. The U.S. firm's compensation is primarily a percentage return on the components it ships to EMBRAER. As the licensee progressively substitutes local content for these imports, the returns will diminish. However, even at 100 percent production in Brazil, Piper still will be paid a fee for service in support of those aircraft. With the exception of those items that cannot be economically produced in Brazil, local substitution is expected to proceed smoothly.

At the present time, the Piper program is basically a licensing agreement; but in the medium and long term, it could provide for the cooperative development of new aircraft. The agreement specifically permits EMBRAER to: (a) fabricate Piper aircraft for sale in the domestic market and, on occasion, to produce jointly with the U.S. company for foreign market sales; (b) replace on a gradual scale Piper-supplied components with EMBRAER-fabricated products; (c) initiate joint programs, sharing development and production of a new aircraft aimed at domestic or foreign markets; and (d) market one another's products through individual distribution networks.

Production capability for the Piper models is being transferred to EMBRAER in three phases. During Phase I, completed structures such as fuselage, empennage, and wings are shipped to EMBRAER for final

assembly and installation of all systems and components. Phase I was
completed for the single-engine models in six months and Seneca is now
also in Phase II. At Phase II, EMBRAER receives structured sub-
assemblies for mating in jigs in addition to the functions achieved in
Phase I. By the third phase, all component parts will be shipped by
Piper for assembly by EMBRAER, followed by three sub-phases: (a)
begin replacement of Piper-supplied parts by Brazilian-made equiva-
lents, including interiors and fifty percent of both fiberglass and acrylics; (b) complete replacement of all remaining fiberglass and acrylics
and produce all harnesses; and (c) produce the aircraft completely with
Brazilian-manufactured parts and components with the exception of
those that cannot be economically produced in Brazil. Upon completion of Phase III(c), EMBRAER projects that from sixty-six to seventy
percent of the Piper aircraft product will be Brazilian in origin, based
on U.S. price.

A comparative look at the specific bargaining stances taken by
Piper, Cessna and Beech in negotiating with EMBRAER provides an
interesting illustration of what is meant by the "accommodators" and
the "non-accommodators" in the area of technology transfer. As mentioned earlier, Cessna enjoyed the lion's share of this rapidly growing
market which, combined with the fact that it operated an extremely
effective distribution system in the country, gave it a slight advantage in
the negotiations with EMBRAER. Anxious to obtain the best possible
terms, however, the Brazilian Government sent a mission to the U.S. to
meet with all the major small aircraft producers and solicit proposals
for a production program in Brazil.

According to EMBRAER, the three principal firms involved (Piper,
Cessna, and Beech) were fully apprised of the "rules of the game." That
is, the Brazilians made explicit their intent to develop their own technical, managerial, manufacturing, and marketing capabilities in small
aircraft production and to reserve the domestic market for Brazilian-
produced aircraft in the future. The latter, it was explained, was not so
much an intent to create a protected industry but an effort to achieve
foreign exchange savings. Implicit in these rules was that, eventually,
only the foreign firm prepared to enter into an agreement with EM-
BRAER would be permitted continued participation in the large Brazilian market.

In the early phases of the negotiations, competition among the
three U.S. firms was spirited, especially between Cessna and Piper.
Beech dropped out as a serious contender quite early, asserting that if
Brazil wanted its aircraft, it would have to import them from its U.S.
facilities. From all appearances, Cessna entered into the negotiations in

complete earnestness, with a preparedness to at least seriously entertain the idea of releasing technology and managerial control to EMBRAER for production of its aircraft. Its ultimate position, however, was not unlike that of Beech's.

Evidence of this was Cessna's refusal to grant EMBRAER authority to make modifications as it deemed appropriate in the Cessna aircraft model the company might choose to manufacture. To one familiar with Brazil's goals in developing its own aircraft industry, such authority would be expected to be a core feature of the kind of industrial cooperation agreement sought by EMBRAER. Cessna's attitude on this suggested its fear that quality or performance standards of its aircraft would suffer if it agreed to this term—a suggestion not lost on the Brazilians and found highly offensive to EMBRAER's sensibilities on this subject and estimation of its own capabilities. A second difference that arose in negotiations between Cessna and EMBRAER concerned royalty payments. EMBRAER wanted no royalty obligation for manufacturing know-how acquired from the foreign partner, and Cessna felt this a legitimate term to the agreement.

Cessna today expresses no regrets that it chose not to accommodate EMBRAER's desired terms to an agreement, in spite of the severe consequences it suffered in the market. As was portended by Brazilian authorities prior to entering into the negotiations, a fifty percent tax (raised from seven percent) was imposed on imported small aircraft in 1975, and importers were required to make a one-year, interest-free deposit to the government covering the full price of the aircraft brought in from abroad. Cessna's sales in the Brazilian market, which in 1973 exceeded 400 aircraft, plummeted to only five in 1976. Cessna has, however, registered strong protest through public channels, such as congressional hearings and press conferences, against EMBRAER's efforts to penetrate the U.S. market, arguing that Brazil must permit comparable ease of access to its own market for small aircraft it if intends to sell its products in the U.S.

Piper and EMBRAER favorably assess their respective experiences with one another, both through the negotiating stages and now in the production phase. Piper attributes this mutual respect to the open and frank approach with which they have dealt with the Brazilians—in addition to the company's early appreciation of the need to demonstrate flexibility on a number of levels. For example, Piper indicates that it recognized the symbolic as well as real importance EMBRAER attached to obtaining authority to modify the chosen models as it felt necessary and readily conceded this point. Any upgrading or improvements which Piper develops in its know-how for these models' production are automatically transferred to the Brazilian partner through documentation sheets and specifications. Two formal meetings are held annually—one in San Jose, Brazil and the other in Vero Beach, Florida—in which EMBRAER and Piper officials air grievances and work out problems.

One important economic benefit which the Brazilian authorities hope to gain by creating a national aircraft industry is the quite significant multiplier effect such a development can be expected to have on supplier industries. (Some forty to forty-five percent of the cost of an aircraft is represented in purchase parts.) Piper has proven to be most accommodating in this area as well, particularly in advising the Government on how best to set up a supplier network for aircraft parts that is responsive to the growing needs of EMBRAER. Piper engineers have also provided on-site training and technical assistance to the component supplier industries. Those items which cannot be economically produced in Brazil, Piper will procure for EMBRAER from its own suppliers.

At present, EMBRAER and its related components industries are not fabricating many detail parts, such as the engine, propellers, radios, or instrumentation. Yet the Brazilians have been fully integrated into assembly of the aircraft kits, welding of airframe parts, some acrylic forming, all of the fiberglassing, all riveting, and nut and bolt assemblies. Piper assesses favorably the speed with which the Brazilians have absorbed the technology and phased local content into production for the model ranges chosen.

It is important to note that there are distinct limitations on Piper's ability to influence many facets of EMBRAER's operations. The marketing of aircraft to domestic purchasers, for example, is a function which EMBRAER has reserved exclusively for itself, despite Piper's well established marketing network in the country. Not only does the Brazilian enterprise insist on performing its own domestic marketing, but also on circumventing the traditional distributorship system through direct factory sales. It is not clear that there is any correlation, but EMBRAER is only recently coming out of a sales slump that it has been in for the past two years. Certainly one contributing factor to the dip in sales has been the extremely tight control the Central Bank of Brazil has held over the available money supply—and the improvement may be attributed to a new program being instituted by the government to assist private entrepreneurs in financing the purchase of small aircraft. It is yet too early to tell whether EMBRAER will be able to sustain this upswing in sales.

Pullman Kellogg's Supply of Ammonia
Technology to PETROBRAS

Kellogg, the engineering and construction division of Pullman Incorporated, is perhaps the most far-thinking and advanced U.S. corporation within our sample, in terms of its preparedness to enter into the new generation of technology transfer agreements. At the same time—partially due, in fact, to its extensive range of experiences in this area—the company has acquired an almost instinctive sense of caution in approaching these new agreements and an acute awareness of the myriad problems they pose. An increasing portion of Kellogg's new markets are developing in the newly industrializing countries, and its management has articulated a most flexible and pragmatic policy for responding to these opportunities.

Kellogg's policy on sharing technology and design-engineering functions with purchaser enterprises was given specific articulation recently at the Second Latin American Petrochemical Congress held in November 1978 in Mexico. Before that forum, company representatives distinguished among three basic progressive steps that may be taken by a purchasing enterprise toward realizing an independent plant design capability. In step one, the process, analytical, and layout phases of engineering are carried out by a foreign contractor. Production design details are done by a local organization with major assistance by the contractor. Step two limits design by the foreign contractor to process and analytical functions only. All layout and production design is handled by local organization with little or no assistance by the contractor. In step three, the capability for independent process and analytical design is achieved by the local organization's engineers.

Kellogg has had direct experience with each of these progressive steps in a variety of LDC situations. It is really only in the "step three" phase of process plant design described above, however, that technology transfer actually takes place. In this phase, the company seeks to provide a local organization with the procedures, coordination, and technology used in plant design through lectures, philosophy, and direct calculations in all the engineering disciplines. Emphasis is placed upon the analytical design functions rather than upon the production design functions. The program includes lectures and design work in the engineering disciplines of process, systems, vessels, furnaces, and exchangers. Excluded, typically, are the production design of foundations, structural steel, piping, electrical, insulation, and similar work.

The particular LDC involvement that we have selected from among Kellogg's vast experience falls clearly within the "step three" phase of process plant design. In a technology transfer contract signed in 1975 with PETROBRAS, Brazil's state oil company, Kellogg agreed to supply Brazil with the know-how, design, and engineering for a series of nine ammonia plants, to be used in the production of synthetic fertilizer—each one slated to have progressively more and more Brazilian involvement. The process know-how of the plants is based upon Kellogg's high-capacity, single-train, all centrifugal ammonia plant design which, since its introduction in the 1960s, has predominated in world markets. Continued upgrading and improvement have maintained this particular process' reputation for reliability and cost competitiveness over the years.

The plants are to be built in the northeast State of Bahia, a region of Brazil which has become the focus of one of the government's most ambitious efforts in industrial planning and integration. PETROQUISA (PETROBRAS Quimica, S.A.), a subsidiary of PETROBRAS, is the coordinating agency for the development of and investments in Bahia, as well as two other so designated "poles" for petrochemical facilities—one located in the Rio Grande do Sul and the other, an older one, located outside Sao Paulo. Kellogg is no stranger to these "poles." The technology transfer agreement represents but one of several projects which it has either underway or completed in Brazil, including three ammonia-urea plants and six catalytic cracking units for installation in oil refineries.

Kellogg figures among the numerous U.S. firms which, wishing to participate in petrochemical development in Brazil, have had to accommodate to the tripartite model devised by PETROQUISA. With the intent to substantially reduce Brazilian enterprise dependence upon foreign partners, the model requires that an equal share of the equity in any new investment be evenly distributed among three parties: the state, Brazilian private capital, and foreign capital. In practice, the requirement that one-third equity be owned by Brazilian nationals often means that the U.S. firm must work with a local partner whose traditional field of activity is other than design, engineering, or the operation of petrochemical facilities, given the relative newness of the industry in the Brazilian economy. The fiscal incentives and protection offered by the presence of a "strong" state partner (PETROQUISA) provide the essential inducements to attract the Brazilian entrepreneur to this field. The government recognizes that without its intervention in this manner, the industry would continue to be dominated by foreign corporations.

As mentioned earlier, Kellogg has already extensively sold its design engineering and process know-how to Brazilian enterprise, yet those contracts were designed primarily to impart an operational capability to the purchaser. The essential distinction in the technology transfer agreement is its intent not only to provide Brazilian industry with nine operational ammonia plants, but, ultimately, to impart to the economy the essential capabilities needed to design and engineer its own plants in the future. A duplicative capability in this highly specialized and complex industrial activity will be achieved only through a carefully scheduled and flexible phase-in of Brazilian participation in all functions of the design and installation of the facilities.

At this time, Kellogg has completed the process design and engineering for only two of the nine plants, but none has actually been constructed yet. The contract assigns primary responsibility to Kellogg, at least for the first few plants, for the process know-how and the process and detail engineering, although the latter will be physically performed in Brazil. Brazilian engineers are being given all basic chemical engineering details, as well as instruction by Kellogg engineers in process design. PETROBRAS has sent twelve of its most promising engineers to Kellogg's engineering center in Houston for ten-month training sessions in basic engineering. The process design being supplied for the plants is the current generation developed by Kellogg, but the contract does not obligate the company to transfer major improvements developed in the process over the course of contract. Minor innovations, such as maintenance or improvements in thermodynamic efficiency, will be incorporated into the Brazilian plant's design.

In contracting to impart detail and process engineering skills to Brazilian nationals in connection with the ammonia-producing facilities, Kellogg is consciously contributing to the build-up of the nation's indigenous capabilities to design and engineer future industrial systems. Many tasks required for the construction, assembly, start-up, and operation of petrochemical facilities can be performed adequately by a number of Brazilian companies. It is in the process engineering, as well as process design, however, that the Brazilian labor force is severely lacking—fields which, once mastered, it is now believed, will provide the critical link between attaining an operative capability in a particular technology and obtaining a duplicative and, ultimately, innovative capability. Kellogg's agreement with PETROBRAS is explicitly designed to assist Brazil to overcome this obstacle and achieve greater self-sufficiency in the petrochemical sector.

The most unusual feature of the contract, in terms of Kellogg's preparedness to accept new terms and conditions for continued involvement in LDC markets, appears in the provision for payment. Implicitly recognizing that Brazil is buying progressively less technology with the completion of each plant, based on the assumption that Brazilian engineers will perform an increasing portion of the functions and acquire greater understanding of the process as each successive plant is completed, the contract calls for payment of the know-how fee at a reducing scale, spread over the period of time during which the plants are being built. The $1 million figure, paid as the lump-sum know-how fee for the first plant, is scheduled to drop to $400,000 by the ninth plant, and the $3 million figure for drawings, specifications, and blueprints will drop to zero.

Kellogg is prepared in this case to accept not only less compensation for its know-how and services as Brazilian engineers accumulate the necessary experience, but also to accept a declining role in the projects by Kellogg personnel, as the functions previously performed by them are assumed by Brazilian nationals. At any stage during the execution of this massive, nine-plant undertaking that PETROBRAS feels competent to go it alone, it can relieve Kellogg of part or all of its duties. After completion of the ninth plant, Kellogg will permit Brazil to duplicate, without additional costs, as many plants as it wishes, but prohibits the licensing of others.

SYCOR's Technology Transfer Agreement
with COBRA, S.A.

Sycor, Inc.[6] is a relatively small mini-computer manufacturer based in Ann Arbor, Michigan. In 1976, the company entered into technology transfer, technical assistance, training and product purchase agreements with Computadores e Sistemas Brasileiras, S.A. (COBRA), a Brazilian computer company owned in part by an agency of the Brazilian Government. Collectively, these agreements commit Sycor to assist COBRA in developing the self-sufficiency necessary to manufacture and market the Sycor 400 series of clustered processing systems in Brazil. This series can communicate with larger computers or can be used as "stand-alone" small business computer systems.

The agreements exempt Sycor from the import controls which today severely restrict the importation of computer products into Brazil and effectively give the company exclusive access to one of the fastest growing mini-computer markets in the world. In the early phases of the relationship, Sycor sold complete systems to COBRA, with an orderly transfer to kit shipments or modules for final assembly in Brazil beginning in April 1978. Approximately $5 million had been obtained by the end of 1978; of this amount, $500,000 represented an advance on royalties and the balance, equipment sales. Brazilian service and installation personnel are receiving intensive training by Sycor in its Michigan facility in the system's software, field engineering, marketing and management. As COBRA acquires greater experience and technological capabilities, a progressively larger portion of the modules will be manufactured in Brazil. In the final phase of the contract, it is envisaged that COBRA will be producing complete equipment.

COBRA was established in 1974, by a Brazilian Government-owned holding company, known as Digibras, in an effort to foster the development of a domestic computer industry. The foreign exchange savings alone that could be realized, if a national industry met some of Brazil's tremendous demand for computer equipment, provided a powerful incentive to the government to foster the industry's development. In addition to easing the balance-of-payments constraints, however, several other objectives are being sought by Brazil through development of a national computer industry. First, government authorities wish to instill an improved ability to use computers efficiently, effectively, and creatively—an ability believed to be best acquired through direct involvement in the design and production of the machines themselves. A second objective concerns the autonomy or independence Brazil could enjoy from foreign manufacturers in making decisions on just how much capacity is needed in its computer installations. The level of investment in and the rate of obsolescence of a computer system, especially large systems, are highly influenced by the product development and marketing policies of the manufacturer. By having its own computer industry, this dependence could be severed and greater efficiencies might follow.

Another and perhaps more important kind of independence that the Brazilians believe can be acquired through a national computer industry is the ability to take on and execute technological decisions as to when an industry is ready to progress to the next stage of production development. A wide cross-section of Brazilian industry, such as aircraft, automotive, petrochemicals, and livestock feeding, has reached a stage of development that requires computerized manufacturing techniques—such as numerically-controlled machinery in an automotive parts plant or an automated processing plant—if international competitiveness is to be attained. It is widely recognized today that computers represent the cutting edge of modern industry. Brazil wants to acquire a self-sustaining capacity to progress in these industries at a speed it feels appropriate and not leave decisions on this rate of progress in the hands of foreign manufacturers.

Sycor's agreement with COBRA is actually Brazil's second attempt at developing a mini-computer industry[7] with foreign technological collaboration. An earlier and quite similar affiliation with Ferranti, Ltd. of the U.K. was unsatisfactory, due in part to Ferranti's inability to service a broad section of Brazilian industry as well as its lack of experience in vertically integrating computer production and thereby proving inadequate in developing the supplier parts industry, which the Brazilian authorities felt to be essential. This second attempt was initiated by COBRA in the fall of 1976 through a series of negotiations held with several U.S. computer companies, for a license to manufacture a minicomputer, to be designated Argus 400.

Aside from Sycor, Data General Corporation was the only other serious contender for the role. In fact, at one point, COBRA appeared to be on the brink of signing an agreement with Data General for its "Nova" technology, but the negotiations broke down over an irreconcilable dispute on ownership rights to the technology. The Brazilian Government required that ownership of the Data General technology— Nova patents, blueprints, and other related matters—be transferred to COBRA at the end of the license period. These terms were unacceptable to the American company which continues to operate a wholly-owned sales subsidiary it established in Sao Paulo in 1975. No orders received since the negotiations with COBRA broke down have been shipped, however, as they are awaiting import license approval by the appropriate regulatory agency, known as CAPRE—Comissao de Coordenacao das Atividades de Processamento Eletronico (Coordinating Committee of Computer Activities).

Data General's unwillingness to accede to Brazilian demands is not particularly surprising, given the company's traditional marketing and production policies. The company is the second largest independent mini-computer manufacturer in the world, and in fiscal year 1976, derived forty-one percent of earnings through export sales. Virtually all of its overseas markets are supplied from U.S.-based production facilities. (The one exception to this practice is a manufacturing license Data General granted a Japanese company for manufacture and sale of some company equipment in Japan.) Approximately 2,400 of the company's 6,000 jobs are related to its export business. Despite the firm's strong international outlook, it chose to forego the opportunity to participate extensively in the growing Brazilian market rather than release its technology to COBRA.

In this decision as well as in its subsequent sense of foul play,[8] the case is similar in many respects to Cessna's in the aircraft industry in Brazil, which we have described above. In both cases as well, an equally competitive and willing alternate U.S. source of the technology existed.

IBM is another U.S. company which felt that it had been offered unreasonable terms by Brazilian development authorities in their determination to build an indigenous computer industry. To ensure that the new Argus 400 product was not immediately overtaken by the stronger, more established and experienced foreign competition, CAPRE developed guidelines for approving any new entrants into the small computer market in Brazil. Priority was given to companies which had Brazilian capital participation and were prepared to transfer advanced technology. Favor was also extended to manufacturing projects that made greater use of Brazilian-made components and did not require massive imports.

IBM's plans to manufacture its new System 32 small business computer in Brazil, announced in 1976, failed to meet these new guidelines. IBM has a policy of generally not associating itself with national investors, insisting upon retaining full administrative and final control of its products. Likewise, the technology transfer requirement was not acceptable to IBM. And, finally, the requirement for low levels of imports posed considerable difficulties for IBM's well-established system of international interchange and production. It appeared to say that the Brazilian authorities were demanding too much in the way of accommodation and departure from their traditional modus operandi, and IBM therefore chose to forfeit the mini-computer market range in Brazil.

IBM do Brasil incurred certain political as well as commercial costs associated with this decision. The Brazilian subsidiary competed vigorously against the company's Japanese and German subsidiaries to be selected by the corporate headquarters as the major manufacturer of the System 32. IBM Brazil has hoped to serve the growing national mini-computer market as well as export markets with the new equipment. To be denied access to its "home" market reflected poorly on its ability to maintain harmonious relations with the Brazilian Government.

IBM's predicament created considerable division and aroused different loyalties within various government and private Brazilian institutions. The more traditional elements of the private sector, as might well have been expected, were skeptical of COBRA's future and, consequently, were reluctant to see IBM excluded from this segment of the market. Bradesco, however, the country's largest private bank, indicated that it would withdraw its financial support from COBRA if the government did not demonstrate its commitment to developing a national computer industry by effectively eliminating the threat of IBM competition. Digibras, of course, advocated protection of the Argus 400, and CAPRE indicated that it felt that direct competition between IBM and COBRA was unrealistic.

In any event, this represented but the first of a long series of difficult questions Brazil will be forced to face as the industry develops. While the extent to which the government is prepared to exclude foreign computer manufacturers from the Brazilian market is yet to be altogether resolved, its commitment to obtain on its own terms the foreign expertise required and to nurture the domestic industry is not open to question.

CASE STUDY—FINANCIAL MECHANISM

Technology Fund

Over the past decade, Brazil has experimented with several technology loan funds to Brazilian enterprises at preferred interest rates and with long-term repayment periods. One of the early funds was established by FUNTEC (Development Fund for Science and Technology), an operational division of the BNDE (National Economic Development Bank). Initially (before 1974), virtually all the funds went to support university research and post graduate assistance. For example, the University of Sao Paulo (USP) was given a $1.8 million grant to develop manufacturing processes for transistors and related micro-electronic devices. The justification for this project was that Brazilian firms could thereby avoid dependence upon a foreign licensing source. Subsequently, FUNTEC attempted to shift support to technical projects submitted by industrial enterprises, but FUNTEC found that there was only a limited range of Brazilian-owned enterprises large enough or otherwise capable of utilizing financial resources for technological development. (See Figure II-2—Sampling of Project Proposals—FUNTEC/BNDE.)

About a dozen private firms, mostly in the electronics and metallurgical fields, eventually submitted proposals requesting funding of from U.S.$100,000 to $1,700,000 for the following: design and develop tape recorder elements and manufacturing processes; design and develop commercial prototype of railroad car to transport cement; establish research center for foundry work; develop economic processing technique for babasu nuts; design and construct pilot plant for the mechanical drying of carnuba (wax) plant leaves; experimental design for telephone apparatus head pieces; develop and improve aircraft crop-dusting techniques; design and construct electronic components for aircraft application (EMBRAER); design and develop new electro-metallurgical casting technique; experimental development for raising shrimp in artificial environment; experimental development of valve-

FIGURE II-2. SAMPLING OF PROJECT PROPOSALS
FUNTEC/BNDE*

PROJECT	ESTIMATED FUNDING COST (U.S.$000)
Design and develop tape recorder elements and manufacturing process.	440
Design and develop commercial prototype of railroad car to transport cement.	Unknown
Establish research center for foundry work.	1,200
Develop economic processing technique for babasu nuts.	540
Design and construct radiation sterilization unit.	490
Design and construct pilot plant for the mechanical drying of carnuba (wax) plant leaves.	220
Experimental design for telephone apparatus head pieces.	260
Develop and improve aircraft crop-dusting techniques.	90
Design and construct electronic components for aircraft application (EMBRAER).	70
Design and develop new electro-metallurgical casting technique.	210
Experimental development for raising shrimp in artificial environment.	330
Experimental development of valvehead used in sinterizing process.	220
Design and construct digital computer prototype.	1,230
Design and construct experimental prototype of two-ton press.	490

*Source: FUNTEC Internal Report—September 1974.

head use in sinterizing process; design and construct digital computer prototype; and design and construct experimental prototype of two-ton press.

The other major example of a government technology fund is one which is jointly sponsored by the State Council of Technology (CET) of the State of Sao Paulo and Development Bank of the State of Sao Paulo (BADESP). The CET/BADESP Fund was initiated with the objective of linking the government and university research and development institutions to production enterprises in industry and agriculture. Specifically, a U.S.$15 million fund was established to finance: (a) applied research and experimental development; (b) purchase of laboratory equipment; and (c) technical and related market information services to small-and-medium industry.

A subsequent similar loan was made by the Inter-American Development Bank in December 1976 for $25 million as part of a $60 million program for Science and Technology Research in Brazil for use by the Financiadora de Estudos e Projectos (FINEP) for: (a) loans to Brazilian business firms for R&D or other technical upgrading programs and assistance; and (b) the developing of R&D infrastructure in the form of laboratory facilities or technical manpower training.

The following are samples of projects funded under the original AID line of credit.

Engenharia Para a Industria Mineral, S.A. (E.I.M.). Two loans amounting to U.S.$312,000 for the construction and equipping of laboratory facilities for mineral ore testing and pilot plant processing in support of design engineering functions—from ore concentration and mineral dressing to chemical engineering of industrial processes.

Piratinanga. Loan for U.S.$99,500 to develop commercial prototype equipment for the processing of vegetable oil and by-products from "babasu" nut. This firm had considerable experience in commercial application of its technical innovations and has already invested substantial effort in the pre-commercial stage of the laboratory prototype.

Enghesa. Loan for U.S.$1,230,000 to develop prototype armored vehicles for the government defense agency and for the export market. The loan was tied to strategic defense considerations for self-reliance in military technology (which also extended to other Brazilian firms engaged in aircraft production). Funds will be used to develop a new type of light-weight armor plate: (a) a nine-millimeter solid steel sheet; (b) a hand-operated gun turret in place of the more complex and costly electronically controlled system; and (c) a newly designed traction system for any trucks. Enghesa was exporting the equivalent of U.S.$12.3 million annually in 1976 in military and commercial vehicles (one of the largest exporting firms in Brazil).

Maquinas Agricolas. Loan for U.S.$182,000 to develop a commercial prototype of a coffee-picking machine. Development based on the U.S. model of a cherry-picking machine. Using a vibration principle through a system of extension arms, the machine automatically deposits beans in sacks under continuous operation. Maquinas Agricolas was an experienced manufacturer and marketer of other mechanized agricultural equipment, such as fertilizer spreaders. Intensified competition from experienced foreign equipment manufacturers in Germany and elsewhere forced the firm to expand its R&D expenditures.

FOOTNOTES

[1] Extended hearings were held by the Brazilian National Parliament in 1977 on the impact of foreign-based multinational corporations upon the Brazilian economy. Testimony was taken on the adverse effects of multinationals, including the pre-empting of large segments of internal markets.

[2] Jennifer Sue Bond and K. Nagaraja Rao, *Governmental Organization and Planning for Science and Technology in Brazil*, Center for Policy Alternatives, Massachusetts Institute of Technology, 1976.

[3] J. Herbert Holloman and K. Nagaraja Rao, *Technological Changes in Sao Paulo and Their Policy Implications*, Center for Policy Alternatives, Massachusetts Institute of Technology, 1976.

[4] *Op. cit.*, footnote 3.

[5] Jose Tavares de Arangjo, Jr. (ed.), *Difusao de Inovacoes na Industria Brasileira*: Tres Estudos de Caso, Instituto de Planejamento Economico e Social (IPEA), Rio de Janeiro, Brazil, 1976.

[6] Since merged into Northern Telecom Systems Corp.

[7] Although Digibras intends eventually to spawn several companies in Brazil, each focusing on a different range of computers, its initial effort in COBRA concentrated on bringing on-stream production capacity in mini-computer equipment. In 1975, the market for this equipment was growing by forty percent a year in Brazil (as opposed to the average mature, industrially-advanced market growth rate of around fifteen percent). In addition, the mini-computer enjoys certain advantages over larger systems as a first time market entry product, from a marketing and servicing point of view.

[8] Data General had informed the Massachusetts Congressional Delegation and the Departments of State and Commerce about its experience with the Brazilians in an effort to publicize what it considers to be a serious national concern for U.S. firms facing increasing and, in its opinion, excessive demands from foreign governments in the area of sophisticated technology transfers. See "Virtual Monopoly Charged in Sycor-Cobra Agreement," *Electronic News*, June 6, 1977, p. 36.

LIST OF ABBREVIATIONS

ABNT	Brazilian Association of Technical Norms
BADESP	Development Bank of the State of Sao Paulo
BDMG	Minas Gerais Development Bank
BNDE	National Economic Development Bank
CACEX	Foreign Commerce Board
CAPES	Ministry of Education and Culture—Agency for the Financing of Graduate Studies
CAPRE	Coordinating Committee of Computer Activities
CBTN	Brazilian Nuclear Technology Company
CDI	Industrial Development Council
CEBRAE	Planning Secretariat—Brazilian Center for Managerial Assistance to Medium and Small Enterprises
CENPES	R&D Center for PETROBRAS
CEPED	Research and Industrial Development Center (for State of Bahia)
CET	(Former) State Council of Technology (Sao Paulo)
CETEC	Minas Gerais Technological Center
CNPq	National Council for Scientific and Technological Development
COBRA	Computadores e Sistemas Brasileiras, S.A. (State Computer Company)
COFIE	Commission on Enterprise Mergers and Incorporation
CONCEX	National Council for Foreign Trade
CONMETRO	National Council for Metrology, Technical Norms and Industrial Quality
CSN	National Steel Company
CTA	Air Force-Technical Aerospace Center
CTP	Proman Technology Center
DIGIBRAS	Brazilian Computer Company
ELETROBRAS	Brazilian Power Company
EMBRAER	Empresa Brasileira de Aeronautica, S.A. (Brazilian Aeronautics Enterprise)
EMBRAMEC	Brazilian Enterprise for Capital Goods
EMBRAPA	Brazilian Enterprise for Agriculture Research
EMBRATER	Brazilian Enterprise for Technical Assistance and Rural Extension
FAPESP	Sao Paulo Foundation for the Support of Research
FIBASE	Brazilian Enterprise for Basic Inputs

FINEP	Financiadora de Estudes e Projectos (Agency for the Financing of Studies and Projects)
FIPEME	Program for Financing Small and Medium-Size Industry
FIRCE	Department of Supervision and Registration of Foreign Capital
FMRI	Fund for the Modernization and Reorganization of Industry
FJP	Joao Pinheiro Foundation
FNDCT	National Fund for Scientific and Technological (S&T) Development
FRE	Economic Reequipment Fund
FUNCET	Sao Paulo Fund for S&T Development
FUNGIRO	Special Fund for Financing Working Capital
FUNTEC	Development Fund for Science and Technology
IBICT	Brazilian Institute for S&T Innovation
IBRASA	Brazilian Investments, Inc.
IFI	Institute of Industrial Development and Coordination of CTA
INDI	Minas Gerais Institute of Industrial Development
INMETRO	National Institute of Metrology, Technical Norms and Industrial Quality
INPI	National Institute for Industrial Property
INT	National Institute of Technology
IPEA	Institute of Economic and Social Planning
IPT	Technological Research Institute (Sao Paulo)
ITA	Technological Aeronautics Institute of CTA
ITEP	Institute of Technology of the State of Pernambuco
MF	Ministry of Finance
MIC	Ministry of Industry and Commerce
NUCLEBRAS	Brazilian Nuclear Enterprises, Inc.
PBDCT	Basic Plan for Scientific and Technological Development
PEB	Special Programs for Loans to Development Banks
PETROBRAS	State Oil Company
PETROQUISA	PETROBRAS QUIMICA, S.A. (Petrochemical Subsidiary of the State Oil Company)
PND	National Development Plan
PNTE	National Program for Executive Training
POLONORDESTE	Development Program for Integrated Areas in the Northeast

PROCET	Program for Science and Technology
PROTAP	Training Program on Management of Scientific and Technological Research
SCCT	Secretariat of Culture, Science and Technology
SENAI	National Service of Industrial Apprenticeship
SEPLAN	Planning Secretariat of the Presidency of the Republic
SICTEX	External Scientific and Technological Information Service
SIDERBRAS	Brazilian Steel Mills, Inc.
SNDCT	National System for Scientific and Technological Development
SNICT	National System for S&T Information
STI	Industrial Technology Secretariat
TELEBRAS	Brazilian Telecommunications Company

CHAPTER III
MEXICO*

INTRODUCTION

There are several compelling reasons why the Mexican Government views a continued expansion of the country's technological base as critical to Mexico's future economic, political and social well-being. Mexico has now reached a stage of industrial development where the improved efficiencies in the use of available resources and installed industrial capacity, which flow from the upgrading of technological resources, are critical to further growth and development and, significantly, labor absorption. Further, the country is now at the point where its economy has largely reached or surpassed the limits of efficient import substitution, and enterprises must improve the design and engineering of products and production cost efficiencies, if they are to further increase value added in domestic markets and expand export earnings through more effective competition in world markets. There are also justifiable political-economic considerations demanding that Mexican enterprises take on a more self-sufficient role in resolving technological adjustment problems in response to a rapidly changing world economy—where it is becoming increasingly necessary to develop new or improved products, more efficient production methods, and new technology to exploit on a cost-efficient basis available raw materials (including energy and mineral resources).

With such a high priority placed on technological development, Mexican authorities have been increasing their involvement in all facets of the expansion of the country's technological base. This involvement ranges from efforts to promote indigenous R&D capabilities at university of other R&D centers to controlling MNCs' involvement in the Mexican economy. The Mexican Government's efforts in this area are being ably assisted by the country's private sector in that there is a growing recognition of the importance of technological upgrading— whether through internal generation or in cooperation with foreign firms.

For MNCs doing business in Mexico the evolving concern with technology upgrading results in increasing demands for a variety of forms of

---

*A list of abbreviations will be found at the end of the Chapter.

technology transfer. The training of local personnel, extensive licensing agreements and joint or controlling ownership are common requirements for direct investment in Mexico. Yet, the Mexican Government has been astutely balancing its demands on foreign firms' technological resources with the propagation of a business environment that continues to attract MNCs.

The two case studies in this chapter explore in detail the type of arrangements which U.S. firms are being required to make with Mexican partners. Included with the case studies is an examination of the Mexican economy's various enterprise sectors, which provides a broader view of the country's approach to the technological component of development.

THE ECONOMY AND TECHNOLOGY

Up to the mid-1970s Mexico enjoyed a rapid economic growth rate, averaging six percent per year, while also maintaining stability in prices and balance of payments. Inflation averaged less than five percent per year. The Government's economic role in this achievement was to carry out direct investments in infrastructure and in key industries such as power, steel, and petroleum, while creating a stable regulatory and institutional framework, as well as good profit prospects, to induce private sector growth. This strategy produced considerable progress and better living standards for many Mexicans.

By 1976 Mexico's real rate of GNP growth had dropped to less than two percent and the economy began to experience increasing difficulties due to public sector deficits, inflation, large balance of payment deficits and capital flight. Yet the most critical problem facing the country related to the rapid growth in population, which reached a peak of 3.5 percent in the mid-1970s. The economy's growth rate was not sufficient to absorb the rapidly growing labor force in productive employment.

Faced with these problems the Mexican Government was forced to adopt a new strategy to revitalize the country's economy. The high inflation rates, large public sector deficits, increasing foreign indebtedness and general lack of confidence in economic management indicated a need for economic stabilization. However, the situation also called for more expansionary policies as economic activity has slowed down, net private investment was virtually non-existent and the gap between new job creation and growth of the labor force was increasing. Fortunately, Mexico's ability to tackle these problems was greatly enhanced through the combination of rich new petroleum discoveries and high world oil prices.

Faced with these conflicting needs and opportunities, the Mexican authorities adopted a mixed strategy aimed at reducing lower-priority public expenditures and increasing public revenues, while proceeding with petroleum and other high-priority investments. The objectives of the Government's program included control of inflation to be followed by a return to high rates of economic growth. An expansion of the country's technological capabilities was seen as critical to a like expansion of the economy. Better management of public sector expenditures, tax reform, more rational pricing and cost control in public sector enterprises, promotion of private savings, limiting wage increases to justifiable levels, and more effective cooperation with the private sector were important parts of the Government's economic strategy.

The Government's new strategy was successful in bringing down inflation and stimulating economic growth in the late 1970s. Favorable oil prospects and increasing capital inflows brought about a rapid increase in imports, reflecting both the resolve to reduce protectionism and the growing demand for capital and intermediate goods as well as foreign technology upon which the expansion of the economy was to depend.

Mexico has the institutional and natural resources needed to achieve her ambitious goals of rapid growth and alleviation of poverty. The challenge remains, though, of how the country can mobilize its resources—its human skills, the institutions, its technological base and its experience—to help resolve its long term development problems. A more detailed examination of several broad areas in which the Mexicans are exerting effort to alleviate these problems follows.

Natural Resource Endowment

The new oil discoveries in 1974 promised to reinstate Mexico to the status it enjoyed early in this century as a major oil producer, if not a major exporter. (This status was lost due to political instability, the discovery of cheaper oil in Venezuela, and utlimately, the nationalization of the Mexican oil industry in 1938.) Prior to the recent petroleum developments in the South, Mexico produced about 360,000 barrels of oil daily from about 4,000 wells, mostly in the Northeast coast of the Gulf of Mexico. Many wells were in the low-yielding bracket.

Then, by mid-1974, forty-eight new wells were operating in Tabasco and Chiapas, each producing an average rate of 5,100 barrels per day, giving a daily total of 260,000 barrels. This brought the total production of petroleum in Mexico as of December 1974 to a volume of 620,000 barrels per day. By December 1976, the number of new wells in the South had increased considerably, reportedly to about 200, and the overall national production can be estimated today in an amount of 900,000 barrels a day.

Under these circumstances, the volumes expected from now on will fall into an entirely different order of magnitude, significantly influencing the entire scope of industrial production in Mexico and of its basic economy. Comparatively speaking, the production of 1974, as based only on the old wells available, had increased four-fold by 1981 as a result of the yields of the new wells.

The natural gas produced in parallel from the new wells is expected to significantly increase as will total gas production. Whereas in 1976, this production was equivalent to eighteen million metric tons annually, by 1980 the production of natural gas reached a level of about thirty million tons. Mexico's production of liquified petroleum gas (LPG) totaled 20.5 million barrels per year in 1976 and reached a level of twenty-eight million barrels in 1980. This will bring welcome relief to the economy as internal demand for LPG has necessitated increasing imports in recent years, especially to serve the northern cities in the East of Mexico and Monterrey, in particular.

Development of Priority Sectors

Sector priorities derive in part from the problems now confronting the Mexican economy: unemployment, trade deficits, capital shortages, the energy crunch, and low productivity in industry (thirty to forty percent estimated idle capacity). Development priorities include the further expansion of basic industries such as steel and petroleum refining, and capital goods and expanded investments in light industries, mining, certain segments of agriculture, and in infrastructure.

In the steel industry, new developments have recurred in the area of the production of blast furnace steel and of sponge iron. It is expected that by 1981, Mexico will have doubled its production of steel over the 1977 level. The new projects are intended to eliminate present supplementary imports of steel and allow for increased exports of iron-based products.

In the energy field, the government is pushing the exploration and exploitation of oil resources as fast and as far as it can. But it is also hoping to derive twenty-five percent of energy requirements from non-oil sources by the year 2000—including nuclear and geothermal sources (recently expanded four-fold to 270,000 kilowatt capacity. Present installed electrical capacity in Mexico is twelve million kilowatts. The government intends to invest $8.1 billion over the next five years in electrical power expansion to lay the basis for the ten-fold increase in power requirement that has been projected over the next twenty-five years.

Investments in light industries are being emphasized because of: (a) the high employment to investment ratio potential; (b) the modest technology and management (production and marketing) demands; and (c) multiple effects in reaching out to large segments of small-and-medium industry.

The emphasis on capital goods industry development derives from: (a) its supporting role to light-and-medium industry expansion; (b) the potential foreign exchange savings; and (c) the upgrading of technical manpower capabilities in the economy.

Export Promotion

Mexico's development authorities recognize that the economy has reached the limits of import substitution, and in order to avoid becoming a "structural pygmy"—like so many developing countries which have persisted with import substitution policies—they have embarked upon a program to make Mexican products more competitive in world markets. The program is also aimed at offsetting Mexico's chronic balance-of-payments deficits. The strategy is essentially two-fold: at the same time that government will be lowering the protectionist barriers to force Mexican manufacturers to improve production efficiencies, it will offer a variety of fiscal incentives to exporters.[1] The devaluations of the peso have enhanced considerably the competitiveness of Mexican products in international markets.

Private Mexican investors, with support from President Lopez Portillo and the backing of the U.S. merchandisers, plan to open more than 850 plants in border-zone and interior industrial parks at a cost of more than $550 million. The Mexican Government expects that by 1982, these plants will be exporting back to the United States finished products estimated at close to $1.5 billion, compared with less than $500 million in 1976. A series of agreements between the government and the private sector called for a huge private sector investment of just under $13 billion and was expected to increase exports and create close to 800,000 new jobs by 1979.

In its stimulation of foreign investment (preferably in the form of cooperative ventures) and acquisition of foreign technology, the Mexican Government is taking pains to direct these activities into a variety of promising export industries. Mexico is intent on using its oil export revenues to broaden the economy and establish major export capabilities other than petroleum. Thus, the Mexican industrialization policies place particular emphasis upon downstream development of petrochemical industries and steel (using national oil and gas resources), upon capital good industries (to reduce the foreign exchange burden and to reinforce domestic product design and engineering capabilities), and upon light industries (to provide a wide array of industrial employment). The National Industrial Development Plan, announced in early 1979, spells out details for industrializing decentralized priority areas, including two industrial port areas on the Pacific coast, and two on the Gulf of Mexico.

The Role of Foreign Investment

The new administration is not in the least apologetic about its recognized need for foreign capital and foreign technology; in fact, it has made explicit a desire to attract foreign investment. At the same time, however, no indication has been made that the authorities are prepared to compromise the legal environment created earlier to regulate foreign investments or transfer of technology. A major difference foreign corporations can expect to encounter is an effort by the government to encourage and promote contractual arrangements that not only are devoid of conditions deemed injurious to the economy, but that also contain measures designed to strengthen the technological and absorptive capabilities of national enterprise.

The foregoing represents significant refinement in Mexico's thinking on how best to use foreign capital and technology for national development in that it suggests an awareness not only of what it *does not* want (as reflected in the two screening registries) but also of what it *does* want. Mexican Government officials want to develop structural relations between the foreign corporations and national firms that incorporate and support this new objective. The Brazilian development model is more efficient in this regard in that it calls for immediate and direct government intervention at the first stages of search, selection and negotiation for technology. As government ownership is rather limited in most Mexican industry—with a few exceptions, such as petroleum—alternative ways must be devised for imparting to the private sector an appreciation that foreign investment and technology should be but the means for enhancing its own technological and managerial capabilities and not simply desired ends in themselves.

The tripartite arrangement, employed so successfully in Brazil to obtain foreign technology and capital on terms advantageous to the economy, is being promoted in select industries by Nacional Financiera,

S.A. (NAFINSA), the government's development bank. Under these arrangements, the government agency puts up substantial capital, supplemented by foreign capital as well as technology, and a national enterprise assumes manufacturing responsibility. At the same time that the Mexican enterprise is acquiring managerial experience, it also obtains the technological know-how in a digestible form so that it ultimately can improve upon received technology as needed.

NAFINSA has selected in particular the capital goods sector as the industry in which to promote the tripartite agreements. Several attractive "packages" have already been prepared for mixed ventures in this field that require one to three years to implement. NAFINSA's programs outlined thus far, however—while important and innovative—seem too modest and discrete to bring about the desired changes on the broad level intended in the structural and substantive relationships between national enterprise and foreign corporations.

To effect such fundamental change is extremely difficult, and legislation in this area is usually of limited utility. Mexican authorities are still searching for a greatly enhanced bargaining power vis-a-vis the foreign enterprise in the form, say, of an enlarged purchasing power domestic market, reinforced by substantial upgrading of national technological and managerial capabilities. Combined, these could lay a firm foundation on which new kinds of relationships would, in most cases, harmoniously develop between foreign and national firms. New programs and policies suggest that Mexico is attempting to lay that foundation, but the overall strategy is as yet vaguely defined and uncoordinated. It will indeed be some time before the strategy reaches down to an operational level.

The Technology Factor in National Development

Since the early 1970s, there has been a concerted effort on the part of Mexican Government authorities to intervene in the technology component of development. The Echeverria administration had strong underlying political motivations to take on a leadership role in the Third World, using the rhetoric of "technological imperialism" and spearheading the drive toward technological self-reliance. In more recent years, since President Lopez Portillo has been in office, the rationale has shifted to a more pragmatic base; but the determination to intervene in the technology component of development has remained, and certain of the instrumentalities originated in the earlier period have been modified and carried over.

The new pragmatism stems from the basic pressures of rapid population growth (at 3.6 percent a year, one of the highest in the world), the lagging ability of the economy to generate new wealth and the resulting unemployment that has plagued the Mexican economy (estimated as high as thirty percent). The Mexican Government recognized that the alleviation of unemployment and the reduction of population growth is a long-term process requiring not only family planning programs, but a further development of the country's economic and technological base. Foreign technology is seen by Mexican authorities as a primary tool in building this base, and U.S. firms are viewed as a primary source of this technology.

Mexican Government policies aimed at reinforcing the demand for domestic technology inputs are aimed at the indigenous development of capital goods industries and support of research, design and engineering infrastructure. In the latter area there is an emerging distinction between the ability to absorb operative technology from foreign sources and the growth reinforcing effects of domestic research, design and engineering capabilities.

Recently, Mexican authorities have been pursuing a policy of seeking to trade access to their oil and natural gas resources for low cost financing and technological support of their industrialization efforts. They have been negotiating with Japan for steel mills, foundry facilities, and steel tubing plants, as well as transportation and port facilities. They have explored other industrial possibilities with France (earthmoving equipment), Sweden (manufacture of turbogenerators), West Germany, and Canada, and the sharing of oil technology with Sweden, Brazil, and Spain.

An important corollary of the foregoing policy thrust is the purposeful effort by the Mexican Government to use its regulatory framework to screen and control foreign investment and licensing contracts and, where feasible and advantageous, to selectively replace or reformulate technology acquired from foreign enterprise that is not providing the full growth thrust needed for the Mexican economy in the form of technological upgrading of Mexican enterprise and maximizing opportunities to expand into world markets. Mexican authorities have found it at times difficult to influence subsidiaries of foreign multinationals in this direction.

It is important to stress that it is not the policy of the present government to progressively exclude foreign enterprise involvement but, rather, to continue to rely upon foreign firms for technological support and entry into world markets with substantive management control yielded to Mexican nationals. In connection with the foregoing, there is a purposeful effort to harmonize regulatory mechanisms with foreign enterprise interest so as to assure a continuing, if not enlarged, but altered role for foreign enterprise.

The new policies in Mexico are attempting to strike a better balance between measures to screen and control foreign involvements and programs aimed at improving the absorptive, adaptive, and creative capabilities of involved enterprise and technical support communities. One set of efforts is in the development of financial mechanisms in support of Mexican enterprise (search for technology, negotiation leverage, and the build-up of technical adjustment capabilities). In the area of supporting science-technology infrastructure, there is a purposeful effort to dichotomize functions and activities between: (a) scientific research and education; and (b) technology search or generation and its application or absorption into productive sectors.

A third policy change is reflected in a shifting emphasis on fiscal and monetary measures, in the form of tax exemptions, export incentives, foreign exchange devaluation, cautious liberalization of protective tariffs, and special lines of credit. They are aimed at encouraging Mexican enterprise to upgrade technology as a contribution to improved efficiency and competitiveness in world markets.

National Policies for Science and Technology

Since 1970, the Mexican Government has assigned high priority to creating an institutional environment that is directly conducive to the controlled and discriminate transfer, assimilation, adaptation, and creation of technology. Prior to that time, the technology factor in national development was not considered to warrant a policy of its own.

The overall objective in national technological development policy today is to develop, in the shortest possible time, national capabilities that permit both technological self-reliance and the enlarged contribution of technological activities to the attainment of economic growth and employment targets. In order to acquire this capability, Mexican development authorities have concentrated on the following sets of activities:

1. Screening of conditions for technology acquired from foreign sources to eliminate restrictive and other disadvantageous clauses from licensing contracts.

2. Regulation of foreign investment to limit foreign ownership and

managerial control and to shield Mexican industry from overpowering foreign presence.

3. Progressive reorientation of the demand for technology toward
   internal sources to optimize development of indigenous design
   and engineering capabilities and capital goods industries.

4. Development of institutional capabilities to search internationally, evaluate, select, negotiate for, assimilate, adapt and generate new technology.

5. Expand training of scientists, engineers, and technicians to move
   from supervised operational roles to management research, design, and engineering functions.

TECHNOLOGY SUPPORT STRUCTURES AND MECHANISMS

Government

The Mexican Government has established a number of institutional
mechanisms and passed certain laws to regulate and promote scientific
and technological development. Each of these mechanisms is summarized and discussed below in the context of its contribution to Mexico's
technology objectives and tactical approach, as outlined in the previous
section.

The National Council of Scientific and Technological Research
(CONACYT) is the central Mexican Government agency responsible for
coordinating and supervising the National Plan for Science and Technology. CONACYT was created in December 1970 to advise and assist the
President in the evaluation, formulation, coordination, and implementation of national scientific and technological policy. The tone as well as
operational reach of CONACYT's activities have gone through at least
two phases since its creation, and the agency is currently in a state of
reorganization and reevaluation of the role it will play in the Lopez
Portillo administration.

Projects undertaken by CONACYT in its first three years of operation—including formulation of the First Science and Technology Plan—
relied exclusively on agreement or interest among the disparate elements of Mexico's science and technology community to participate in
projects. This approach corresponded to the pluralistic philosophy on
which CONACYT was founded. The majority of these projects aimed at
strengthening the then weak links of research institutes with higher
education and the productive sectors.

Three types of participants were involved in these early activities: (1) the research user, which could be an industry, a public agency, or in general, any individual or legal entity that needed research undertaken; (2) a research institution comprising one or more research centers; and (3) CONACYT in the role of coordinator. From the tripartite arrangements and activities, increased demands were expected for basic as well as applied research. Improvements in the use of resources available to research centers and the promotion of interdisciplinary work were also expected. Due to a lack of clearly defined priorities and objectives as well as dependence on the immediate interest and entirely voluntary involvement of participants, this approach did not permit much opportunity for coordinating national science and technology functions; nor did it achieve enduring links between production and research units.

Mexico's science and technology policy was considerably strengthened in 1974 with the decision to give priority to the establishment of indicative programs. These programs constituted a first effort to rationalize resource allocation and support given by CONACYT to research projects. Indicative planning had been initiated earlier, but with little official commitment. The indicative programs were viewed as sectoral planning, promotion, and budgeting mechanisms to create strong, permanent relationships between the generation of knowledge, technical innovation and diffusion.

The indicative programs consist of policy guidelines for the scientific and technological community and the users of technology. Responsibility for management and definition of program content, under the auspices of CONACYT, was assigned to a Program Committee composed of representatives from research, government, education, and private institutions. Ten indicative programs are currently in operation and a number of others are projected. There are existing programs for national nutrition, demographic research, tropical ecology, scientific research and educational techniques, health, science and technology for agricultural development, use of marine resources, use of mineral resources, and meteorology.

Other activities assigned to CONACYT in support of national research and technological development proposals include: (a) financial support of scientific programs; (b) developing Mexico's science and technology infrastructure by providing equipment and personnel; (c) offering legal assistance to investors who wish to patent their innovations; (d) commercializing innovation in collaboration with the Mexican Foreign Trade Institute; and (e) providing information to companies on alternative sources of technology (see INFOTEC, below).

The National Scientific and Technological Planning Commission

(COMPLANCYT) is a multisectoral committee composed of representatives from each sectoral program committee. COMPLANCYT has the
following responsibilities: (a) to formulate strategies and policies in
support of scientific and technological development; (b) to evaluate
ongoing programs; (c) to make recommendations on the use of the
Federal Budget in support of science and technology; and (d) to coordinate planning for science and technology. The Inter-Institutional Scientific and Technological Commission (COMICYT) was created to over-
see the budgetary aspects of the National Science and Technology Plan.

In accordance with the above objectives, the following are matters
of concern to the Mexican authorities and, therefore, of regulation:
acts, contracts, and agreements effective in the country and related to
the concessionary use or exploitation of trademarks and patents; the
supply of know-how; the provision of basic or detailed engineering or
technical assistance; and company operating and managerial services.
The National Registry for the Transfer of Technology (RNTT) was
established under the Ministry of Industry and Commerce with authority to review all such matters. Its staff undertakes a technical, legal and
economic analysis of the contracts to ascertain whether the conditions
and prices under which technology is acquired are in agreement with
the legal stipulations.

The cases in which an act, contract, or agreement will not be accepted for registration are as follows: for technologies which are easily
acquired within Mexico; when the price bears little relation to the value
of the technology or constitutes an unjustified or excessive burden on
the economy; when lawsuits that arise over the interpretation or enforcement of a contract are to be submitted to foreign courts for resolution; when the duration of a contract exceeds ten years; when the
technology supplier imposes restrictions or limitations on the purchaser
regarding exportation, production, personnel, use of complementary
technologies, research, management, free acquisition of equipment,
parts, tools and raw materials, sale of manufactured goods, etc., or
where the purchaser is obliged to cede to the supplier any patents,
trademarks, innovations, or improvements obtained or made by him.

Technology Registry

In 1972, the Law Governing the Registry for the Transfer of Technology and the Use and Exploitation of Patents and Trademarks was
passed. It represented the first indication of unequivocal intent of the
Mexican Government to intervene in negotiations between national
firms and foreign technology suppliers. The regulations were drafted

with several purposes in mind, the most important ones being: to regulate technology transfers so that their contractual conditions promote
national development objectives; to strengthen and reinforce the bargaining leverage of the national enterprise; to impress upon the national
entrepreneur the contribution technology can make to the country's
development; and to establish an official register where the contractual
conditions of technology transfer arrangements can be monitored and
associated problems identified.

In determining whether contracts contain any of these prohibited
conditions, the RNTT must make several qualitative and quantitative
judgments. The economic evaluation of contracts is based on cost studies in other countries, financial analyses of the records of the purchasing company, and prepared estimates of impact on the Mexican economy. The technical evaluation is based on comparative studies of processes and products, technical bibliographical studies, visits to the
companies, world information on patents, and specialized technical
information from data banks and information services in the country
and abroad.

As of March 1976, close to 7,000 contracts were submitted for
review, of which half (approximately 3,500) were certified as complying with the law and were registered. A major cause of registration
denial was excessive payments. Other causes in order of frequency: (a)
excessive duration of contract validity (forty-two percent of rejected
cases); (b) limits on production levels or fixing of sale and resale prices
(forty-one percent); (c) unjustified and excessive payments (thirty percent); and (d) submission of arbitration to foreign courts.[2]

Mexican Government officials feel that the law on technology transfer has served as an effective vehicle for redressing some of the in-
equities Mexican firms have suffered in their dealings with foreign corporations. The Ministry of Industry and Commerce reports that the
application of the law and the functioning of the Registry have not
only eliminated restrictive clauses from contracts but have also permitted significant savings to be realized in payments for royalties, technical assistance, and engineering and other services—calculated on the
basis of the life of the contracts at about U.S.$254 million up to July
1976.

It is generally believed by both the public and private sectors in
Mexico that the Registry has boosted the bargaining leverage of national firms in negotiations, although it is yet too early to know its
precise impact in this area. The Registry has had a positive effect on the
balance-of-payments current account; on production costs of some
goods manufactured under license; on the rationalization of imports of

raw materials, intermediate goods, and machinery and equipment by promoting the diversification of suppliers; and on broadening export possibilities by eliminating export prohibitions. The enhanced bargaining leverage derived from the regulations has been perhaps of greatest benefit to small and medium-sized firms due to their comparative weakness in managerial, technological, and financial resources. Larger Mexican firms as well, with considerable expertise in searching for, selecting and purchasing technology in world markets, have also managed to obtain move favorable contractual terms with the law's support and leverage. Furthermore, the RNTT has collected valuable information on company experiences, the characteristics of transferred technology, and the conditions prevailing in other countries similar to Mexico with regard to these matters.

The major disadvantage the RNTT operates under is that it intervenes primarily *ex post facto*, i.e., after the Mexican enterprise has initiated and, frequently, concluded the negotiations for acquiring foreign technology. Its participation as a legal and regulatory instrument is practically non-existent in the more difficult stages of the technological process, such as, for example, the selection of the technology, its adaptation to the size of the Mexican market and the supply of resources and factors of production, or the development of a local technology.

Foreign Investment Registry

In February 1975 criteria were established for the authorization of foreign investments in the Law to Promote Mexican Investment and Regulate Foreign Investment. Prior to the passage of this law, foreign investment in Mexico was governed by a series of disjointed and uncoordinated laws and regulations, adopted over a number of years, which reserved for the state certain economic activities, permitted exclusive Mexican investment in others, and otherwise imposed limits and conditions on foreign capital. Between the late 1950s and the early 1970s, several conditions obtained in foreign investments that were considered disadvantageous and undesirable for the economy. First, there was a trend among foreign investors to move away from establishing new manufacturing companies and toward acquiring already established operations, thereby displacing Mexican capital which was then rarely reinvested in productive activities. Moreover, some strategic industries, such as automotive, chemicals, pharmaceuticals, rubber and paper, as well as others that had been satisfactorily run by Mexicans, e.g., tobacco and food, increasingly came under the control of foreign companies.

Furthermore, by the late sixties, a significant amount of foreign capital was invested in commerce and services—activities of minimal contribution to the national economy. During this same period, foreign investors began tapping national financial resources for supporting new investments and continuing operations. This practice placed them in competition for capital with Mexican firms and aggravated balance-of-payments problems. And, finally, it was widely believed that the activities of foreign investors were not making sufficient contributions to the national development goals, such as employment-generating export expansion[3] and strengthening indigenous technological capabilities.

The Law to Promote Mexican Investment and to Regulate Foreign Investment sought to consolidate and integrate all previous, related laws and regulations and to establish the sectors in the conditions under which foreign capital could be invested in the country. In spirit, the law accepts foreign capital only as a minority partner with national capital, and diminishes its impact on the country's development. The sectors reserved exclusively for the state are petroleum and other hydrocarbons, mining of radioactive minerals and the generation of nuclear energy, certain other sectors, and public utilities (electricity, railways, radio, and telegraphic communications). Only Mexican capital can participate in radio and television; urban, inter-urban, and federal motor transport and national air and sea transport services; forestry; and the distribution of gas.

Regarding foreign investment, the law limits foreign capital to forty percent of investment in secondary petrochemicals and the manufacture of automotive components and to thirty-four percent of investment in the exploitation of national mineral reserves. In sectors where the law or other dispositions have not established a maximum percentage, "foreign investment can participate in a proportion which does not exceed forty percent of the capital and where it in no way controls the management of the company." There are exceptions to this law, however. Certain firms, such as General Electric, which invested in Mexico during an earlier period are usually permitted to retain their equity holdings, but are intermittently urged by the Mexican Government to divest to a minority position.

Two instruments were created by the law which affect technology policy: the National Foreign Investment Commission (CNIE) and the National Foreign Investment Registry (RNIE).

The CNIE is responsible for regulating foreign investment, formulating national policy on these matters, and implementing the law. It coordinates public sector actions in these matters and establishes criteria and requisites for the application of legal standards relating to foreign investments. CNIE staff includes engineers, lawyers and econo-

mists who review as many as 100 projects per month. In authorizing
foreign investments and establishing the conditions that should be
adopted, seventeen criteria and characteristics are taken into account.
Among these criteria are the technological contribution of the project
to the national economy, use of nationally manufactured components,
and the employment and training of Mexican technicians.

Authorization is required from the CNIE in cases where the foreign
investor intends to acquire more than twenty-five percent of the equity
or more than forty-nine percent of the fixed assets of an established
company; or when companies with a majority of foreign capital wish to
install new establishments and produce new products. New companies
which did not exceed the maximum percentages permitted by law did
not require authorization. Consequently, it is largely those companies
which seek to establish themselves with percentages of foreign capital
greater than those stipulated in the law that require authorization for
the CNIE.

In the period immediately preceding and following the bill's passage, considerable controversy and fear were aroused that the new law
would be used to limit rather than regulate foreign investment. These
fears, however, have largely proved unfounded for, despite the revolutionary rhetoric that accompanied its passage, in practice, it has been
managed and interpreted by officials favorably disposed to both the
private sector and foreign investment. The final version of the bill did
not contain the more radical proposals originally supported not only by
government officials but by prominent Mexican businessmen and bank-
ers as well. The latter group later reversed its position, fearing that the
bill would prove the start of a broader process of economic control of
industry, and lobbied successfully for more moderate legislation.

In effect, the Law on Foreign Investment simply confirmed the
traditional "rules of the game" which MNCs played by investing in
LDCs, with significant exceptions in terms of ownership. The law established the principle of majority Mexican ownership in new foreign investment projects. In addition, the law has made it possible to limit the
acquisition of Mexican-owned companies, and in cases in which the
CNIE has had to authorize the investment, the association of national
and foreign capital has been urged where feasible, with advantageous
conditions for the country's economy being the primary negotiation
objective. Nevertheless, the explicit technological objectives contained
in the law have largely gone unrealized. Benefits gained during negotiations for CNIE authorization have been limited to securing from some
multinationals a commitment to carry out labor training programs and
a reduction or elimination of royalty and technical assistance payments
in some contracts.

The response of U.S. firms to Mexico's foreign investment law is varied. There appears to be a cross-section of U.S. firms which have successfully entered into minority joint ventures, shared their technology and in some cases assisted the Mexican affiliate in exporting goods to the U.S. Among the firms which have experienced difficulties with the new law are the previously mentioned foreign firms which have retained majority ownership in spite of the forty-nine percent ruling. The Mexican Government has generally refused to allow these firms to expand their programs and/or facilities in Mexico.

Law on Inventions and Trademarks

In February 1976, the Mexican Congress passed legislation designed to reform the national industrial property system. The new legislation, entitled the Law Governing Inventions and Trademarks, substituted for the Law Governing Industrial Property which had been in effect since 1942. In introducing the legislation to the Mexican Senate, the then Secretary of Industry and Commerce, Jose Campillo Sainz, characterized the 1942 law as following "the philosophic principles of the liberals of the past century" which were no longer acceptable and called for a new "law to regulate the rights of inventors and the use of trademarks which is in accord with public order and social interests." In addition, the Mexican Government felt it was imperative that the law on industrial property conform with those on the transfer of technology and foreign investment.

The basic innovations in the law with respect to patents, in comparison with the 1942 law, were the reduction of the term of enforcement of the patent from fifteen to ten years, the suppression of patentability in certain areas of industrial activity, the strengthening and simplification of the system for compulsory licenses, the introduction of licenses for causes of public utility, and the creation of a totally novel institution in Mexican law called "certificate of invention."

With regard to trademarks, the basic changes were that the law expressly protects service trademarks, suppresses the special non-use renewal of trademarks, expands the concept of non-registrable trademarks, authorizes the public administration to make use of trademarks mandatory in certain industrial activities or prohibit such use, and establishes the obligation of associating foreign trademarks with Mexican trademarks.

The Research Community

Although far from self-sufficient in technological capabilities, progressive efforts are being made to expand and enlarge indigenous capabilities. The National Institute of Scientific Research (INIC) was created to support basic and some applied research in selected fields. During the last decade, INIC's activities expanded considerably to include promotion of linkages between basic research and the productive sector. National expenditures for R&D increased eighty percent between 1960 and 1973, and the number of research institutions during that period increased by a third. A little over one-half of R&D is sponsored by the federal government, a large share of which is carried out in universities. There appears to be scant attention paid to applied R&D except in the research centers sponsored by CONACYT and the Ministry of Industry which are intended to feed results into the private sector.

The Mexican Technical Research Institute (IMIT), created by the Bank of Mexico, and the National Industrial Development Laboratories (LANFI) are two government bodies which are especially attuned to the problems of small to medium-sized firms. LANFI, CONACYT, and the Ministry of the Presidency have recently created three research and technical centers which will assist in the development of local and regional industries. These centers provide assistance in organization and administration, quality analysis and control, development and adaptation of appropriate technologies, and technical information systems (supported by INFOTEC).

INFOTEC, originally established within CONACYT, is currently a semi-independent and partially self-supporting agency. Seventy percent of its operating cost is covered by the Mexican Government and the rest is derived from the sale of technical services. INFOTEC is a unique combination of an industrial extension system and a technical information service. Its operative system demonstrates that technical information can be mobilized: (a) to develop new product lines; (b) to redesign existing products; and (c) to design and engineer products for manufacture appropriate to the firm's scale of operations, capital resources and machine operator skills. INFOTEC may be especially useful to the small and medium-sized firms which often do not have the in-house capabilities necessary to solve many of their technological problems.

The successful functioning of INFOTEC depends upon trained and experienced staff, willingness of the client to fund at least a portion of expenses, and an entrepreneur mentality among INFOTEC staff attuned to this type of service.

INFOTEC is experiencing some difficulty in obtaining the funding and support necessary to carry out its functions. Specifically, funds are needed to hire and retain trained personnel and to improve the IN-FOTEC collection of technical information. Outside of the question of funding, INFOTEC has had problems in finding indigenous personnel who have the professional experience needed to provide the varied types of technical assistance requested by the private firms. Especially scarce are individuals with design/engineering capabilities. One possible remedy for this situation which INFOTEC is considering would be to hire foreign engineers on a temporary basis to provide technical advice and to train Mexican engineers.

In addition to the above-named organizations, there is a considerable number of specialized research institutes associated with a given industry, such as the Mexican Steel Research Institute (IMIS) in steel and the Electric Industrial Research Institute (IIIE) in the electrical field. Other industry-related institutes are: IMP for the petroleum and petrochemical industries, the leather research institute, the equipment and maintenance research institute, the packaging and container research institute, and the metal-mechanical research institute. The Ministry of Industry plans to create more such institutes. Although staffed by competent, well-experienced engineers and Mexican scientists, these institutes, partially funded by CONACYT, generally lack effective linkages with industrial enterprises.

One exception to the foregoing observations is the Mexican Petroleum Institute (IMP), which has shown considerable proficiency in acquiring engineering capabilities and in sustaining effective linkages with the petroleum and petrochemical industries. IMP operates on an annual budget of $25 million. The Institute has designed a large number of PEMEX plants (relying on foreign firms for assistance in the more complicated processes), and earns approximately $2 million annually in royalties and technical service fees.

Prior to the founding of IMP, technical services in the areas of exploration, exploitation, refining, transportation, and distribution, of petrochemicals were almost completely provided by foreign firms. IMP has gradually acquired its own capabilities in technical services, adapting foreign technologies through the use of its engineering staff and by training its personnel at plant sites (in the public and private sectors). IMP has already registered eighty patents with the Mexican Government (most of them processes adapted from foreign technologies not covered by patent rights).

Only a small portion of all projects (eight percent) is conducted exclusively by IMP staff. Many projects are carried out in cooperation with U.S. research institutes, universities, and design/engineering groups such as Kellogg, Lumus, and Universal Oil Products (UOP). Of fifty-seven new petrochemical plants or expansions constructed between 1970 and 1974, only two cases of basic engineering and twelve of detailed engineering were carried out by Mexican companies. In 1975, however, all detailed engineering in ongoing petrochemical projects was being done by Mexican engineers, in collaboration with foreign technicians.

The Financial Community

The government-funded Nacional Financiera (NAFINSA) is the principal economic development bank in Mexico and, with the exception of the Central Bank of Mexico, handles the largest volume of indigenous resources. In its lending programs, NAFINSA's main objectives are: (a) increasing employment and income; (b) promoting regional development and industrial decentralization; (c) encouraging exports; (d) strengthening productive enterprises; (e) promoting domestic savings; and (f) encouraging national economic independence.

NAFINSA implements the above objectives through various specialized development trust funds which it administers. Included is the National Fund for Industrial Development (FOMIN), which offers support particularly to small and medium Mexican enterprises for new or enlarged industrial facilities. FOMIN emphasizes regional development, decentralization, import substitution, and export promotion. Industries receiving the most financing are food products, chemicals, metal goods and machinery, wood and cork, and cement.

The Guarantee and Development Fund for Small- and Medium-Sized Industry (FOGAIN) provides financial and technical assistance to small and medium industry. In 1975-76 FOGAIN authorized 2,732 loans to 2,399 companies, amounting to more than $100 million. The productive activities receiving the most financing were food products, textile manufacturing, shoes, clothing, chemicals, and metal goods. The National Preinvestment Studies Fund (FONEP) offers financial and technical assistance to investors to carry out feasibility studies on proposed projects or undertake regional and sectoral studies.

The Industrial Equipment Fund (FONEI) was created by the Bank of Mexico to extend loans to firms which produce exportable products or import substitutes. FONEI principally provides funds for fixed assets and/or feasibility studies. FOMEX, also under the direction of the Central Bank, is another Mexican Government program which attempts to promote exports. From 1975 to 1976, FOMEX financing increased by fifty-four percent, and in 1979 it increased by another fifty percent, reaching $600 million. Principal emphasis will be placed on the export of manufactured goods.

The Mexican Society of Industrial Credit (SOMEX) is a government-owned, profit-making corporation which offers credit to industry and other productive enterprises to further Mexican economic development. It is composed of commercial banks, mortgage banks, a stock exchange and investment funds. SOMEX has been particularly effective in contributing to the development of the automotive, chemical and petrochemical, and capital goods industries.

SOMEX's activities involve: (a) granting loans and credits for the purchase of raw materials, machinery and equipment, and contracting for construction of industrial plant facilities; (b) capital investment for the incorporation, expansion and consolidation of business enterprises; (c) preinvestment surveys, project evaluation and design engineering plans; (d) low-interest loans for businesses which qualify for credit from federal funds; and (e) provision of technical services or actual management of an enterprise.

The principal criterion SOMEX applies in investment decisions is the projected rate of return. In assessing an application for funding, SOMEX conducts market surveys and supervises in-depth feasibility studies to determine the profitability of the investment. The targeted rate of return is around fifteen to eighteen percent. MNCs are frequently selected for investment because their technology is competitive, they are willing to put up additional capital and they have access to world markets. Many U.S. companies, such as Amoco, Celanese, Pittsburgh Plate Glass, American Motors, as well as French and Spanish companies, have shared in SOMEX-sponsored ventures.

The financial community in Mexico actually provides minimal support of the nation's technological development objectives. Except for SOMEX and NAFINSA, which is now engaged in a cooperative program with the United Nations to assist Mexican enterprises in their technological acquisition activities, there is little refinement in financial mechanisms to reinforce the search and selection process or to assist Mexican firms in the more effective utilization of the technology component.

In 1979, FONEI negotiated a $5 million line of credit from the World Bank to finance the technological upgrading of Mexican enterprises. This new fund, the Industrial Technology Improvement Fund (ITIF), was designed to respond to the new needs and conditions of the Mexican economy. It provided for direct loans to Mexican enterprises to finance new or improved product or process development, or investments in people, facilities, and equipment to carry out these activities.

The rationale behind the new fund from the Mexican Government's viewpoint was that Mexican enterprises must play a more self-sufficient role in resolving technological adjustment problems in response to a rapidly changing world economy—where it is becoming increasingly necessary to develop new or improved products, more efficient production methods, and new technology to exploit on a cost efficient basis available raw materials, including energy and mineral resources. Technological adjustments were seen as needed and sought as contributors to: (a) increased productivity and competitiveness in world markets; (b) new, unexploited industrial employment opportunities; and (c) foreign exchange earnings or savings.

The design of the new financial mechanism was based on a survey of a cross section of Mexican enterprises to determine both the technical needs of these firms and the projects they were likely to undertake. Information was also developed on the sources from which these enterprises had obtained the product and process technology they had in hand at the time of the survey. All three sets of information were used in the design of the fund, particularly the categories of loan funds to be made available.

The companies surveyed ranged from a fairly large division of an even larger conglomerate with sales of nearly U.S.$300 million and employing several thousand people to small enterprise units with sales under $500,000 and employing fewer than 200 people. (See Figure III-1, column 2.) The products produced by surveyed firms ranged from spices and frozen citrus fruits to specialty steel products and equipment for oil rigs (see Figure III-1, column 1). Some produced a wide range of products, while others specialized in the production of a single line. The technological capabilities varied greatly among the enterprises surveyed—ranging from firms with substantial research, development, and engineering capabilities, to firms with minimal staff and capabilities to resolve technological adjustment problems.

The principal sources of industrial technology acquisition mentioned by surveyed firms were: (a) comprehensive licensing and purchase agreements with various foreign industrial firms; (b) assistance from both foreign and domestic engineers and technicians; (c) the training abroad of the company's Mexican technicians; and (d) in-house research, design and engineering efforts. (See Figure III-1, column 3.)

The main needs for technical assistance that were cited by surveyed firms include: (a) new or improved product designs; (b) new or improved equipment and process design-engineering; and (c) improved quality control procedures. Several companies were producing supplies for rapidly developing domestic industries and had to meet the continually changing demands of their markets. (See Figure III-1, column 4.)

Proposed solutions for which the surveyed enterprises would presumably use the ITIF funding included: (a) the use of in-house design and engineering groups to develop new products and production processes; (b) the negotiation of technical service agreements with foreign industrial suppliers of operational technology; (c) technical information searches and training of Mexican technicians abroad; and (d) visits by foreign technical experts to advise on product-process-equipment design and engineering problems. (See Figure III-1, column 5.) The amounts of funding needed for the cited projects ranged from under $100,000 to near $15 million. (See Figure III-1, column 6.)

It was evident from the survey that technological adjustments of the kind proposed under ITIF were of high potential benefit to the Mexican economy, but that they generally involved added risk from the commercial standpoint, as compared to buying packaged technology from tried and tested foreign sources. Consequently, there was an economic justification for a slightly lower interest rate based on the potential public benefit to be derived from the added commercial risk. One insight that emerged from the survey was that R&D managers in most firms need all the outside support they can get to induce management to take the inevitable risks involved in developing new technology.

The survey results also indicated that the firms most appropriate for ITIF project financing were enterprises with in-house capabilities to diagnose and resolve technical problems, and those dependent upon outside sources to diagnose and resolve technical problems (as distinct from seeking package solutions from foreign sources). Inventors or new enterprise groups with technical innovations needing development were considered too high a risk for ITIF to undertake.

The following categories of expenditures were designated as eligible for funding:

1. Research, design, or engineering projects involving adjustments in product or component design, new or improved production methods or 'materials processing, new or improved equipment design, experimentation with new industrial materials, or other related RD&E activities.

2. Training of Mexican engineering or technical personnel abroad, including visits to industrial plants, research laboratories, or other industrial technical facilities, or for specialized training in applied research fields in foreign research institutes.

3. Visits to Mexico by foreign technicians and engineers to advise on solutions to technical adjustment problems; to train research, design, or engineering personnel to find solutions to technical problems; or to provide other technical adjustment support services.

FIGURE III-1. SURVEY OF MEXICAN FIRMS' TECHNICAL NEEDS AND PROPOSED PROJECTS

(1) PRODUCTS MANUFACTURED	(2) 1977-78 SALES (U.S. $MILLION)	(3) SOURCES OF TECHNOLOGY	(4) TECHNICAL ADJUSTMENT NEEDS	(5) PROPOSED PROJECT	(6) ESTIMATED COST (U.S. $MILLION)
1. Steel and electric cables for oil rigs and related applications.	20-49	Have developed own direct-reduction process for sponge iron.	Improved production of sponge iron and increased gas efficiency.	Purchase equipment and materials to improve production processes.	10-15
2. Steel and electric cables for oil rigs and related applications.	20-49	Know-how for first electric-mechanical cable from British Ropes (U.K.).	Develop a new electric-mechanical cable for oil exploration. Improve production methods and quality control on existing product lines.	R&D project to include technical literature search, and visits by Mexican engineers to foreign facilities.	1-2
3. Over 100 different industry chemicals from petroleum derivatives.	Under 1	Technical know-how from engineering training in Stanford and Cornell Universities.	Machinery and know-how for production of additional petrochemical products.	Use own staff to design-engineer process and equipment for new product groups.	Under 0.5
4. Electric conductors and cables.	50-100	Know-how, equipment, and materials from Canadian and U.S. firms.	Improved production technology in high-voltage, high-tension cables.	Negotiate new license agreement with Sweden or Japan.	0.5-1.0
5. Oil pumping systems.	1-9	Original technology from U.S. firms.	Develop a new type of hydro-dynamic, deep, secondary oil recovery system.	Use own design and engineering team to carry out technical studies and to design and construct first prototypes.	Under 1 0.5-1.0
6. Machinery for the glass industry, glass-molding equipment and plastic injection machines.	20-49	Original technology from British and U.S. firms.	Design of higher volume and multi-purpose glass and molding machinery; improved furnaces, materials, and special glass design.	Train Mexican technicians abroad to participate in new research, design, and engineering projects.	1-2
7. Packaging materials and containers.	10-19	Equipment and materials from France.	Design new families of packaging materials, including plastic laminates.	Technical information search, possible visits and training of Mexican technicians abroad.	Under 0.5
8. Aromatics and spices.	10-19	Developed own technology under technical services agreement from Sweden.	Improved methods for extracting raw materials. New processes for manufacturing food derivatives.	Technical information and foreign market search. Technical services agreement with foreign manufacturer.	Under 0.5

9. Flat and structural steel, specialty steels, and sponge iron intermediaries.	Over 500	Have developed own direct reduction process for sponge iron.	Improved production of sponge iron and increased gas efficiency.	Purchase equipment and materials to improve production processes.	Over 10
10. Frozen citrus fruits.	1-9	Process and equipment design from IMIT (Mexico); technical assistance from U.S. lab.	Higher volume production methods, improved waste disposal and quality control; newly designed equipment for sorting fruit.	Use IMIT and local equipment firm technicians to redesign process and equipment.	Under 0.5
11. Pumps, tanks, winches, and masts for oil rigs.	50-100	Manufacturing licenses from various French and U.S. firms.	Design four new lines of oil well rigs (2000 to 4000 meters) including drilling heads and mud-pumping equipment.	Use own design and engineering group to design and construct first prototypes.	5-10
12. Manufactures engine cylinder heads, and other automotive components.	1-9	Production know-how from visits to American plants.	Adapt equipment and methods to new materials and component designs.	Visit U.S. and German plants. Hire foreign engineer for a year.	Under 0.5
13. Low-cost housing systems and light-weight aggregates for building materials.	(No sales as yet)	Own product and process, supplemented by visits to American plants.	Develop commercial prototype product and pilot plant facility.	Contracted with IMIT to help design pilot plant facility.	Under 0.5
14. Paints, ceramics, batteries, leaded glass, and petroleum derivatives.	20-49	Technical assistance from American and Japanese firms; also in-house R&D facility.	Development of new products and materials processing technology.	Use own RD&E staff to design products, redesign process and equipment, supplemented possibly by Mexican technicians visiting foreign facilities and foreign expert visits to Mexico.	Under 0.5
15. Paper from bagasse.	(No sales as yet)	Intend to adapt original process developed by Colombian subsidiary of U.S. firms.	Design of an economically efficient small scale plant to process sugar cane bagasse into Kraft paper, with modular design feature so facility can be enlarged when demand increases.	Use own engineering group to design facility. Purchase foreign equipment to build prototype plant.	3-5

4. Purchase of technical information (drawings and specifications for manufacturing equipment, materials processing, or product designs); quality control or testing equipment; or other tangible hardware needed in the technical adjustment process, including pilot plant construction.

5. Technology audits and world market scanning services for new product developments and equipment designs of the type carried out by INFOTEC. FONEI may even suggest a technology audit in borderline cases involving firms with limited experience in diagnosing and resolving technological adjustment problems.

The Enterprise Community

Public Sector (PEMEX). Petroleos Mexicanos, the largest public sector enterprise in Mexico, is considered to be the most dynamic of Mexico's state-owned enterprises. PEMEX currently employs 800,000 individuals and produces 765,000 barrels of crude oil per day, of which approximately one-fifth is exported (ninety percent to the U.S. and ten percent to Israel). PEMEX officials anticipate that production will nearly double by 1982. PEMEX currently operates 1,600 drilling rigs, more than any other oil company in the world. In 1977, the government oil company was allocated $4.7 billion, slightly more than forty-six percent of government investment in the industrial sector.

PEMEX employs modern petroleum techniques and is considered by many to be a pioneer in Latin American petrochemical production. Since the Mexican oil expropriations of 1938, the international oil companies have avoided investing in the Mexican petroleum industry. As a result, PEMEX has become nearly self-sufficient in petroleum technology, project engineering and equipment design. In fact, PEMEX has exported certain of its own petroleum technologies to other countries, including the U.S. (one export is a desulphurizing process used by two U.S. firms).

The Lopez Portillo administration views accelerated petrochemical production as an important element in achieving long-term economic growth in Mexico. A PEMEX spokesperson estimates that production of basic petrochemicals will leap from the present four million tons/year to fifteen million tons/year by 1982. For some time, PEMEX has been producing primary petrochemicals (olefins and aromatics), having constructed some of the largest ammonia plants in the world. Now, PEMEX is expanding into secondary petrochemicals such as acrylonitrile and ethylene. Thirty plants are currently under construction, nine of which are large-scale operations geared for export production.

Interaction with foreign companies has been a vital element in developing the Mexican petrochemical industry. PEMEX has been very successful in negotiating with these firms for the acquisitions of new technologies. In constructing its first acrylonitrile plant, PEMEX undertook a joint venture with British Petroleum (BP), rejecting the more sophisticated but expensive SOHIO technology. The second acrylonitrile plant was also built in conjunction with BP, with assistance from the Badger Corporation. PEMEX expects soon to have the technological expertise needed to build the third acrylonitrile plant without foreign assistance.

In constructing its first 450,000 metric ton ammonia-urea plant, PEMEX collaborated with Kellogg, purchasing low-density, polyethylene from Imperial Chemicals, Inc. (ICI) of the U.K. Other plants under construction include a 1,110 million ton ethylene plant (the world's largest), for which PEMEX will purchase all basic and detailed engineering (except ovens) from Lumus. PEMEX itself is doing all the design/engineering for the 500 million cubic foot gas trigenic oven for this ethylene plant, which will recover gas and freeze-keeping methanes through cryogenics.

In contracting the above agreements with foreign companies, the policy of PEMEX is to negotiate what are essentially licensing agreements with foreign firms, in which they purchase the "black book" which provides information on the technology, detailed engineering specifications, and patent rights. Basic engineering services frequently must be purchased outside Mexico, because of the high indigenous demand for these services. The apparent preference for licensing arrangements on the part of PEMEX underlines its determination to learn quickly from foreign companies and become self-sufficient in petrochemical production. PEMEX is striving to become competitive in world markets, and is gearing its plant production to exceed domestic demand so that an active export industry will eventually emerge.

PEMEX has been quite successful in recruiting university-trained people for its operations. It has also been adept at on-the-job training and in retaining the personnel it employs. Top PEMEX staff is generally hired from within the company, resulting in opportunities for upward mobility which gives incentives to workers. PEMEX employs more than 6,000 university-trained engineers, many of whom leave PEMEX temporarily to acquire some experience in the private sector, to return later. The combination of effective utilization of human resources with a wise investment policy has been a major component in the success of PEMEX.

Small and Medium-Sized Enterprises

In spite of the Mexican Government's propensity to favor large-scale, capital-intensive investment, there has been some awareness of the need to support small-to-medium-sized industry. Thus far, however, there has been little growth in engineering services, technical assistance, and extension services for small-to-medium-sized industry. As in other Latin American countries, this segment of the enterprise community is generally weak in its ability to plan its own technological strategy, to generate new technologies (with the exception of limited adaptation), to search and negotiate for new technologies, and to conduct its own training programs (with the exception of on-the-job training).

There are several Mexican Government agencies which are especially oriented toward assisting smaller enterprises in fulfilling the functional capabilities that are so difficult to achieve on a small scale. For example, many activities of INFOTEC are geared to firms which have not had the in-house capabilities to solve their own technological problems and to select and acquire new technologies. Another government entity which is oriented to smaller firms is FOGAIN, part of NAFINSA, which provides financial and/or technical assistance to small and medium-sized industry.

Several research institutes, such as IMIT and LANFI, are also designed to accelerate the growth of local and regional industries. The previously mentioned research and technical assistance centers created through the collaboration of LANFI, CONACYT and the Ministry of the Presidency are attempting to help this group. The centers provide many types of technical assistance, such as organization and administration, quality control, research, adaptation of technologies, and technical information. Expansion of such activities for small-to-medium-sized industries may be a viable policy alternative.

Private Sector Enterprise. This subsection of the enterprise community in Mexico is composed of: (a) Mexican-owned conglomerates; (b) Mexican-controlled joint ventures; and (c) foreign-controlled joint ventures. All three groups have developed advanced capabilities in the search, selection and negotiation functions of technology acquisition and varying degrees of ability in performing the remaining functions.

The large Mexican conglomerates, while limited in number, exert a powerful influence on the national economy. In many instances, they have demonstrated a strong capability in generating new or adapting foreign technologies, but they usually find it more expedient and ultimately cheaper to fill technological needs from foreign sources. While some technical assistance and training is required from the technology supplier, their own support capabilities are well developed and quite adequate.

A Mexican-controlled joint venture is usually the result of a "Mexicanization" process whereby the foreign subsidiary merges with an already established, national enterprise in the same or a complementary industry. Effective control over management, marketing, and production is usually transferred to the Mexican partner and, to the extent its capability permits, technological decisions can also be taken by the national enterprise. Most of these firms, however, have not yet developed sophisticated in-house R&D capabilities and will continue to rely upon the foreign partner for its more advanced know-how. Considerable joint R&D does take place, however, strengthening national technological capabilities.

Foreign-controlled joint ventures result from cases where a subsidiary is Mexicanized through the sale of majority equity to national investors. Virtually all technology is acquired under license from the parent corporation. Basic decisions regarding product design and production capabilities reside with the U.S. partner. The foreign-controlled joint venture is very competent in acquiring and using foreign technology, but this capability rarely extends to an understanding of the basic design and engineering required to produce the technology.

Comparisons and Overview of Mexican Enterprise Community

The functional tasks associated with the technology component of production and marketing systems are listed in Figure III-2, and the relative capabilities of Mexican enterprise groups noted accordingly. State-owned enterprises and the larger Mexican-controlled or U.S. affiliated enterprises have substantial planning capability. In the case of U.S.-controlled firms the basic decisions on product design and production capabilities reside with the U.S. partner. The latter also rely almost exclusively on the U.S. parent for the research generating and technical support and managerial training functions. Mexican-controlled joint ventures rely heavily upon their foreign partners as a technology source.

In the generating of technology (product design and process engineering), state-owned enterprises and wholly-owned Mexican enterprises have demonstrated emerging capabilities. Small and medium-sized Mexican enterprises must rely largely upon equipment and materials suppliers or foreign licensors for production know-how.

Small-to-medium-size Mexican firms are at a particular disadvantage

FIGURE III-2. EVALUATION OF ENTERPRISE CAPABILITIES
IN MOBILIZING TECHNOLOGY COMPONENTS

FUNCTIONAL TASKS	STATE-OWNED ENTERPRISE (PEMEX)	MEXICAN-CONTROLLED JOINT VENTURE (IEM-Resistol)	U.S.-CONTROLLED JOINT VENTURES (DuPont-Carbide)	WHOLLY-OWNED MEXICAN CONGLOMERATE (DESC, Cydsa, Grupo Alfa)	SMALL-MEDIUM MEXICAN ENTERPRISE
PLANNING • Policy Coordination • Project Formulation	Excellent planning capabilities; are aware of which technological needs are unfulfilled and are attempting to bridge gaps.	Mexican partner has substantial share and capability in strategic and operational planning.	Mexican partner has little or no choice in strategic decisions involving technology.	Substantial capabilities to formulate technology components of production programs.	Planning limited to choices of technology from a limited range of supplier sources.
GENERATING • Research • Development • Design Engineering	IMP, in conjunction with PEMEX, has been successful in generating sophisticated petroleum technology, some of which is licensed abroad.	Rely on U.S. partner for substantial portion of technology, but have some R&D capability to vary product range and design.	Rely almost exclusively on U.S. partner for product process design and plant engineering.	Emerging capabilities to design and engineer technology segments, including products and processes. Particularly motivated when denied alternative.	Limited capabilities to develop or adapt own technology.
SEARCHING • Technical Information • Licensing Sources	Adequate capability, especially in petrochemicals.	Have significant capability to find and evaluate alternative technology.	Little or no need to go outside corporate family for technology.	Substantial capabilities to seek out technology alternatives when motivated.	Contacts generally limited to equipment suppliers and licenses.
NEGOTIATING • Technology Acquisition	Has shown considerable proficiency in dealing with foreign companies.	Have capability and retain options to negotiate technology alternatives.	(See above.)	High level of competence in negotiating for technology packages reinforced by Registry. Some firms believe laws inhibit negotiations.	Limited ability to search for technology or leverage to negotiate.
SUPPORTING • Standards • Quality Control • Extension Services	Adequate capabilities but some reliance on foreign firms in petrochemicals.	Majority of support services from U.S. partner but also have in-house and domestic support facilities.	Most support services delivered through U.S. partner's "umbilical cord."	Partial reliance on foreign licensors and domestic labs and equipment-material suppliers.	Inadequate support structure within firm; need outside assistance.
TRAINING • Professional • Managerial • Technicians	Both IMP and PEMEX conduct training programs; some reliance on foreign firms for more advanced techniques.	Management and technical training from U.S. partner but significant in-house and domestic capability.	Rely heavily on U.S. partner for management level training.	Substantial in-house training and resources to fund outside activities.	Mostly on-the-job training of machine operators.
USING • Installation • Operation • Maintenance	Adequate capability to maintain and service directly or through technical services contracts.	Substantial operational capability derived in part from U.S. partner.	Substantial capabilities to absorb and maintain delivered technology.	Substantial capabilities to utilize and maintain installed technology.	Considerable dependence on technology suppliers in making technology operational.

in the search and negotiation for technology—their contact sources, once again, limited largely to equipment and materials suppliers. State-owned enterprises and the larger, wholly-owned conglomerates and Mexican-owned joint ventures have substantial capabilities in this area, although their orientation or the need for technological self-reliance covers a fairly broad spectrum.

In training and technical support services, state-owned enterprises and the larger Mexican-owned firms and joint ventures are in a strong position. The wholly-owned conglomerates place a stronger emphasis upon the development of management capabilities to command the technology component, including the abilities to make technological decisions and carry out technological adjustments and/or innovation programs.

Small-to-medium-sized enterprises are dependent to a considerable degree upon licensors and equipment-material suppliers for quality control, material specifications and other operational elements in the use of technology, particularly as changes in market conditions occur. The larger Mexican enterprises, state and private, have substantial capabilities to absorb and maintain delivered technology.

ENTERPRISE SECTOR CASE STUDIES

In the material that follows, we have divided experiences into three distinct enterprise groups, according to the extent of Mexican ownership and managerial control of the particular firm. The first set of experiences we analyze are those of large, wholly-owned Mexican conglomerates. The second and third sets of enterprise configurations are variations on the foreign subsidiary. In the second set, we look at foreign subsidiaries which have Mexicanized in both the spirit as well as letter of the law on foreign investment. That is, in addition to holding a minority position in equity, both managerial and, to the extent possible, technological decisions have been yielded to Mexican control. In this set as well, Mexicanization was largely achieved through a merger with an already established Mexican manufacturer, thereby enhancing national technological capabilities. The final set of experiences concerns enterprise configurations composed of foreign subsidiaries which have Mexicanized in the letter of the law only. While the foreign subsidiary in this case may have had to sell off majority equity to Mexican nationals, effective managerial and technological control remains in the hands of foreign corporations.

WHOLLY-OWNED MEXICAN CONGLOMERATE

A handful of Mexican-owned and -controlled enterprises—most of which originated as family-run companies—have grown and diversified to become powerful elements of the economy. Not only have they been extremely influential in national economic and commercial affairs, but they also carry considerable weight in Mexican politics. The top-level management of these companies have served in various government ministries, held ambassadorships, and sit on the boards of a host of other Mexican and foreign companies. The more recent generations of the family enterprises have received their professional training at the most prestigious and highly regarded business schools in the United States and Europe. This is all by way of saying that the officials of these companies hardly fit the American stereotypical image of Mexican businessmen.

Among these national corporations, or groups as they are called, perhaps the largest and most powerful is the Grupo Alfa, with headquarters in Monterrey, which serves as the operating base for several other important Mexican industrial groups. (One frequently hears them referred to collectively as "The Monterrey Group" and usually in a respectful tone.) Grupo Alfa began as a small family-run steel company, Hylsa de Mexico, S.A., and later became involved in the bottling and container industries that grew up around Monterrey. Diversification continued as the company acquired a wide range of both Mexican and foreign firms, and today, Grupo Alfa owns and manages twenty-six companies. The pattern of diversification was designed to create a triangular structure with the three angles representing banking, insurance, and industry. This base allowed for effective and well-coordinated vertical integration.

The first foreign company bought out by the Grupo Alfa was Philco. Its general practice is to purchase the company and allow the original management to run the operation for a short period of time, after which it moves in its own people. The group enjoys a proven record in management and management of technology. For years, it has had excess capital to invest in new or already owned facilities. Its technological and marketing capabilities are substantial, having developed next-generation process technology on its own.

When a company of Grupo Alfa seeks foreign know-how, it brings considerable expertise to the search and selection process, and in negotiating with the technology supplier, it bargains from a strong position derived from financial resources, share of the national market, export potential, and a high absorptive capability. In light of the generally favorable position they hold in dealing with foreign corporations, it is probably unlikely that Grupo Alfa companies, unlike the smaller Mexican firms, have found their bargaining leverage considerably enhanced by the new laws on technology transfer and patents and trademarks.

In fact, there is some suggestion that Grupo Alfa and other large Mexican conglomerates view the laws as obstacles or constraints to their operations, under certain circumstances. For example, the company may be prepared to accept certain restrictive conditions or to pay a higher price in order to obtain a particular technology it deems necessary. Commercial expediency may sometimes overrule government-proposed terms and conditions supportive of national development objectives. One observer of the Mexican economy and business community indicated that some of the problems associated with the large Mexican enterprises, such as Grupo Alfa, may ultimately be less manageable from the Mexican Government's perspective than the problems caused by the foreign corporations. According to this individual, government officials are aware of this possibility, but feel it is first necessary to gain some degree of control over the foreign companies.

A second firm we wish to discuss in the context of large Mexican enterprises and their relationship with foreign firms is the Epsna Manufacturing Company, a producer of oil exploration and field equipment, such as Christmas trees, pumping units, high pressure valves, and centralizers. Epsna's annual sales volume is in the range of $2 million to $4 million, of which ten percent is exported. Its major client until 1965 was PEMEX, but problems arose, and it became necessary to diversify and develop new markets.

Epsna's diversification program was based on several licensing agreements it negotiated with foreign companies. Technology for gas compressors was purchased from a Dutch company; an agreement with the U.S. firm, Swanson, for the manufacture of overhead cranes is pending final negotiation, and Epsna has entered a third round of licensing with the Gray Tool Company of Texas for the manufacture of heavy equipment, including compressors and pumps for industrial use. One of the most attractive features of the latter arrangement is that Espna can use Gray's worldwide marketing facilities to sell its products. In 1975, it entered into a joint venture with Gardner of Denver, Colorado, and is now manufacturing compressors, rock drills, and forty-five-ton slush pumps which Gardner then markets in the U.S.

That business with PEMEX was no longer strong enough was not the only reason compelling Epsna to diversify. As is the case with all capital goods industries, diversification is essential in order to balance out world market demand cycles and to accommodate import restrictions. Even the larger firms often find themselves spread too thinly as they move from manufacturing one product to another, but the smaller ones experience real difficulties in coping with the changes in design, materials, and processes.

Drawing on their experiences in negotiating for technology with foreign firms, the management at Epsna made some interesting, if not particularly informative observations. In general, it found American companies easier to negotiate with than Europeans, being more flexible and realistic. European firms were characterized as officious, more avaricious, and reluctant to agree to modest projects, preferring large, long-term contracts. Another trait that made Europeans less popular with this company was their insistence on exacting a penalty when a contract was cancelled due to economic problems.

What is informative, however, is Epsna's observation on how best to attract foreign technology on favorable terms; i.e., make it worthwhile for the foreign associate. For example, its licensing agreements with Gray Tool Company permit the latter to sell non-Jewish content products from Mexico to Arab countries and also allows it access to LAFTA (Latin American Free Trade Association) markets for products which would otherwise be denied to a U.S. exporter. Epsna had also been approached by a Japanese enterprise interested in setting up a manufacturing operation in Mexico to serve the U.S. market. The proposed export items were specialized fine wires and tire metal cord belts, both of which have high labor content (e.g., raw materials represent only ten percent total content in the specialized wire rope, as compared to thirty-five percent for high volume items). The Japanese firms would thereby realize considerable savings in transportation and labor costs and avoid U.S. import barriers imposed on Japanese products. Epsna is actively seeking new companies with which to manufacture items for export whose production is no longer economical in the U.S.

Epsna's own R&D capabilities are quite sophisticated, but it has a strong preference for obtaining the technology it needs through foreign licensing. Its experience has been that to purchase know-how is easier, cheaper, faster, and ultimately more profitable than to develop it on its own. At one time, the company tried unsuccessfully to obtain a license from Anaconda for a difficult teflon-coated conductor manufacturing process. It was forced to develop its own technology through a long, arduous process, but the Mexican firm now licenses a British associated firm, Bector, to manufacture the cable and supply them with the wire.

Epsna's mode of diversification differs from Grupo Alfa's in that it obtains new manufacturing capabilities through licenses with foreign companies rather than through acquisition. Their attitudes toward enhancing their own indigenous technological capabilities, however, are not dissimilar in that neither firm would choose to undertake R&D to generate a new technology, unless it was inaccessible to them. This is generally the case despite evidence that both have substantial capability in this area already. Undoubtedly, however, their ability to search, select, and negotiate for technology is stronger than their R&D capabilities, and their desire to rapidly acquire proven know-how takes precedence over an interest in enhancing their own technological abilities. This attitude is understandable from the enterprise viewpoint, but it represents a real dilemma that Mexican development authorities must grapple with in attempting to upgrade national technological capabilities.

A third Mexican-owned firm we shall examine is Cydsa, S.A., the Sada family conglomerate, which today has twenty subsidiaries and is included as a member of the "Monterrey Group." It has three main product lines—synthetic fiber, chemicals and petrochemicals, and film—and in 1976 had a sales volume equivalent to well over $200 million of which about three percent is exported.

Cydsa's corporate policies toward technology appear to be aligned with the articulated national goals in science and technology. It feels it is ready and wants to make certain fundamental process design decisions on technology it acquires from abroad. For example, if it is necessary to reduce the temperature in a particular process, it wants to be able to choose among alternative chemical materials and techniques. Cydsa's efforts to obtain control, in particular, over process know-how have thus far had varying degrees of success. It was unable to duplicate a chlorine process obtained under license due to cost and safety problems, but its engineers have acquired considerable expertise in handling quality control problems. Cydsa acknowledges that it is still highly dependent on the licensor to help solve most technical problems.[4]

Cydsa management recognizes that the mere purchase of a particular technology through licensing will not give them the kind of understanding needed to develop even an operative capability in the technology, much less a duplicative or innovative capability. With this in mind, they entered into negotiations several years ago with ten different foreign firms (Monsanto, Mitsubishi, and eight other Japanese companies) for synthetic fiber technology. In addition to wanting an internationally competitive process, the Mexican firm also wanted ongoing technical assistance and training, the assignment of two or three engineers from the licensor company to its facility, the understanding that it could freely seek advice from time to time from the licensor, and that payment be linked to production units rather than take the form of a lump-sum. Most important, Cydsa wanted "unbundled" technology, that is, the opportunity to acquire the discrete elements of the fiber process as it determined its readiness to absorb and use them, or until such a time as it felt capable of proceeding on its own.

Of the ten firms contacted, Monsanto was Cydsa's first choice, based on the belief that they shared compatible, if not similar, business outlooks and that communication would be facilitated through proximity and language. Once negotiations began, it became quickly apparent that this belief was without foundation. Monsanto insisted upon providing only "packaged" technology and demanded a lump-sum payment to be spread over a five-to-ten-year period. Mitsubishi proved to be the more amenable source of technology. Mitsubishi's technology was the very same offered by Monsanto, as the former had acquired the Monsanto process in 1958 and, under the terms of the contract, was free to use or license it elsewhere. During negotiations, the Japanese firm was open-minded to Cydsa's expressed needs and preferences for the project. The signed contract called for payment in the form of royalties only, based on units of production as well as ongoing technical assistance. Know-how is transferred at a speed and in a form determined by Cydsa.

In 1976, the agreement was expanded to include a new "high crimp" fiber technology developed by Mitsubishi which at present represents the most advanced and competitive process available. (Mitsubishi's process for the particular fiber is reputed to be one-third the cost of all other competitors.) An important advantage Cydsa now sees in dealing with Japanese firms is their ability to scale-down the production process to accommodate the smaller Mexican market and at the same time remain cost-competitive. It has been Cydsa's experience that American firms think in dimensions too grand for Mexico, whose market is only ten to fifteen percent the size of the U.S. market.[5]

A second, brief illustration of Cydsa's experience in negotiating for technology with foreign companies concerns its search in 1959 for rayon tire core know-how. DuPont was its first choice, presumably for reasons similar to its initial preference for Monsanto in the synthetic fiber case. The terms Cydsa sought were also similar in this instance. DuPont's demand for a $1 million flat fee, however, forced the Mexican firm to a European source. The final know-how agreement, with a Dutch firm, called for a more moderate three percent royalty on production over a ten-year period.

Cydsa's officials acknowledged that these unhappy experiences with U.S. firms may be dated and that the latter have become more accommodating to Mexican enterprise needs in recent years. They noted though that American companies are still reluctant to buy Mexican equipment and balk particularly at employing Mexican basic and detailed engineering, even when it means suffering severe cost disadvantages.

The Cydsa experience is significant both in terms of Mexican technological development objectives and U.S. corporate attitudes. The conditions under which it seeks to acquire foreign technology support national goals to reduce dependency on foreign suppliers and to strengthen the indigenous technological and design/engineering capabilities. Cydsa's refusal to compromise the terms on which it acquires foreign know-how, even if it entails accepting its second or third choice supplier, indicates that the often inflexible stance taken by U.S. corporations is ultimately self-defeating. This is particularly true in light of the proliferation of internationally competitive and aggressive foreign technology suppliers and the advanced level some Mexican firms have reached in performing the search, selection, and negotiation functions.

The last Mexican group we shall look at is known as DESC, the acronym for Desarrollo Economico Sociadad Civil, an industrial promotion and development group. DESC is not an enterprise itself, but rather is a management and financial holding company, which has equity in, and provides managerial support to, the Mexican operation of several multinationals. The original concept and founding of DESC is credited to Manuel Senderos—President of his family's company, Comermex, the country's largest banking and insurance firm—who felt a strong need in Mexico for an effective instrument for promoting new investment and employment opportunities in the country.

In 1967, Mr. Senderos and a group of Mexican businessmen bought control of Negromex, the Phillips Petroleum subsidiary, a producer of carbon black and synthetic rubber. Controlling interest was acquired soon thereafter in a second subsidiary, the Dana Corporation's Spicer operation which manufactures axles, piston rings, and other automotive parts. Their intent was to divest themselves in these operations to a maximum of one-third of total equity and sell these shares to the Mexican subsidiary or other Mexican interests so as to guarantee national control of the enterprise. The capital gains taxes they were obligated to pay as Mexican principals upon divestiture were prohibitively high and severely eroded their ability to continue operating in this way. Senderos and his primary partner, Antonio Ruiuz Galindo, brought to the attention of high level government officials, including Lopez Portillo who then was serving as Secretary of the Treasury, the tax obstacles the group faced in their efforts to Mexicanize foreign companies. The result of these talks was the passage in June 1973 of the law called Sociadad de Fomento which permitted DESC to incorporate as a legal investment company.

Once DESC achieves majority Mexican ownership of an industrial concern, it then assumes responsibility for supervision and support of the company's management. It becomes involved in the day-to-day operation of a company only when a major problem arises. Its staff is small (approximately thirty-five people), but is composed of highly qualified specialists in finance, insurance, manufacturing, management, and engineering. It is essential to DESC that it project a strong image of professionalism, and DESC officials attribute its success to its core professional management capabilities. This professional and comparatively impersonal approach represents a marked departure from the traditional and predominant family form of business in Mexico.

A major benefit that companies enjoy through association with DESC is an enhanced credibility and weight in consultations with Mexican Government officials on national economic policy. For example, the DESC Group collectively will be able to guarantee an export level equivalent to nearly $90 million in 1977, and this gives them considerable influence in government decisions regarding the extent and nature of export incentives. In addition, banks extend loans and lines of credit more readily with the knowledge that the company is a member of the DESC Group.

Virtually all manufacturing technology used by members of the DESC Group is obtained from foreign corporations. (Monsanto, Dana, Hercules, Phillips Petroleum, Robert Bosch, and SKF are the major foreign suppliers of the DESC companies' know-how.) DESC officials feel that the experiences of their companies in negotiating for technology dispel the widely held belief in Mexico that national enterprise development has been thwarted by the exploitative and abusive practices of the MNC. They acknowledge that successful negotiation for technology on favorable terms requires considerable technical, legal, and financial expertise, but that it can be and has been done. The crucial element, in their opinion, is careful selection not only of the most appropriate technology for the task, but of the foreign supplier as well.

DESC officials cited the relationship between Negromex and Phillips as exemplifying a compatible and successful partnership. When technical problems arise, an open-door policy allows Negromex engineers to seek advice from Phillips' Oklahoma laboratory or to request on-site assistance. The flexible arrangement also permits Negromex to obtain additional know-how as it feels necessary to remain competitive.

The astuteness the large Mexican conglomerates bring to the search, selection, and negotiation process may be advantageous from the commercial and financial point of view of the enterprise. This astuteness, however, may not be advantageous to the Mexican economy in the long run or supportive of national technological development objectives to achieve indigenous design/engineering capabilities and the ability to generate internationally competitive technology.

MEXICAN-CONTROLLED JOINT VENTURE

A variety of means are available to the foreign subsidiary operating in Mexico to comply with the national law on foreign investment. A first and major objective of the 1973 law was to subject foreign capital to national control. Important but secondary considerations were to place managerial and technological decisions taken by the enterprise in Mexican hands, thereby enhancing and reinforcing indigenous capabilities in these areas and achieving progress toward national self-reliance in industrial manufacturing.

Only a limited number of foreign corporations have chosen to Mexicanize in a manner supportive of the latter set of objectives, but among those that have gone in this direction, their experiences have been largely favorable. The motivations compelling three foreign subsidiaries to Mexicanize in this fashion are discussed below, along with their respective relationships with their Mexican partners, and subsequent experiences in enhancing their technological capabilities.

In 1950, Monsanto Mexicana, S.A. was established as a 100 percent owned and controlled subsidiary for the manufacture of polyvinylchloride and polystyrene. In 1958, the Mexican Government enacted the Chemical Regulatory Law requiring majority Mexican ownership in all chemical firms operating in the country. Monsanto was not compelled to Mexicanize at the time as the law was not retroactive. For the next decade and a half, Monsanto continued operating as a foreign subsidiary.

Toward the end of this period, it began experiencing some subtle and some not so subtle pressure from government authorities to Mexicanize. Monsanto's applications for permits to expand or diversify production were turned down; other necessary official approvals were processed slowly or temporarily postponed. The "writing was on the wall" for this large and very traditional U.S. multinational, and a three-year study was begun by the company that weighed the costs and benefits of Mexicanizing and explored various alternative ways of complying with the national law.

During this same period, a Mexican company, Industrias Resistol,

S.A., was searching for a foreign manufacturing partner to upgrade and diversify production in order to alleviate its unfavorable credit situation, which was due to large inflows of capital the company received from U.S. banks in the early seventies. Resistol was a large Mexican firm of the prominent Patron family and a manufacturer of adhesives, paints, and some industrial chemical products.

Industrias Resistol had been (and still is) extremely successful in manufacturing industrial and home-use adhesives. The company developed the adhesive technology on its own, and the manufacturing process is considered revolutionary in the industry. Astute marketing efforts have made Resistol adhesive the most commonly used in Mexican shoe and other factories, and its glue is widely distributed in the nation's public schools.

With the advice and assistance of DESC (discussed in the preceding section), Monsanto and Resistol began talks in 1972 to form a joint venture. DESC at this time had taken an interest in Resistol, the company's Chairman was DESC's founder, Manual Sanderos, who thought it would be particularly advantageous for the Mexican company to diversify into polystyrene production. In the proposed joint venture, Resistol was only able to afford forty percent equity in Monsanto. The Monsanto Corporation on the other hand, felt that its purposes in entering the joint venture would not be served unless its share dropped to forty percent—the then prevailing equity position taken by new foreign entrants to the chemical manufacturing sector in Mexico. An equity formula was worked out for the joint venture (which took Resistol's name) whereby Monsanto owns thirty-nine percent; DESC, thirty percent; Industrias Resistol, thirty percent; and one percent is placed on the stock market.

The merger with Resistol has permitted Monsanto to expand its production capabilities and to diversify into new product lines. Between 1972 and 1975, profits of Industrias Resistol have soared by over 200 percent, and sales have increased by almost 150 percent, much of which were to export markets. A large volume of its industrial phosphates are shipped to Chile, and a substantial portion of its polyvinylcholoride production is exported to the U.S. and other foreign markets. The Mexican partners of the concern have found their competitiveness increased through the infusion of newer, more sophisticated technology, provided by Monsanto. In addition, the financial structure has been strengthened through DESC and Monsanto capital.

Monsanto's traditional corporate policy of retaining its most competitive technology in owned and controlled subsidiaries, however, remains unchanged. This policy in Mexico is based as much on its belief that it has virtually no protection under the new patent and trademark law as out of fear that its Mexican partners may gain a competitive edge. The products of Industrias Resistol, by comparison with Monsanto's most advanced technologies, represent a standard range.

This situation may reduce the competitiveness of the joint venture's production in world markets, and therefore foreign exchange earnings, but it does not necessarily affect the extent to which national design/ engineering capabilities are strengthened by the joint venture, given the Mexican partner's stage of technological development. In addition, managerial decisions regarding production, marketing, and to a considerable extent, choice of technology are controlled by Mexican nationals. This kind of arrangement represents the kind of mutually beneficial relationship that the Mexican Government is encouraging between national enterprises and foreign corporations.

A second Mexican-controlled joint venture we shall discuss is that of Industrias Electricas Mexicanas, S.A. and Westinghouse Electric Co.— known as IEM. From 1948 to 1973, Westinghouse had operated in Mexico as a wholly-owned subsidiary. Recognizing that a continued harmonious relationship with the Mexican Government was necessary to its operations, it Mexicanized in 1973 by merging with IEM and taking a minority equity position (forty percent).

IEM operates ten business groups. Forty-two percent of sales is derived from the manufacture of capital goods (motors, transformers, circuit breakers, and other heavy electrical machinery); thirty-five percent from home appliances (TVs and audio equipment); and twenty-three percent from construction of retail stores and the production of elevators and air conditioners. (It was necessary that the company move into the latter group during the recession to offset substantial sales losses in its traditional product lines.) When Westinghouse moved out of home appliances in 1974, IEM took on another manufacturer partner, Mitsubishi, in order to continue in this product line.

Largely employing Westinghouse technology, IEM is now moving into high technology areas, and has recently begun two important expansion projects. One concerns the development of extra-high-voltage and large-capacity transformers and the other involves the design and construction of sophisticated, automatic control systems for the process industries. IEM has created a new company, Silectra, S.A., to run the latter project, with forty percent participation by Westinghouse and sixty percent of IEM. If the project is successful, it will be the first time that automatic control systems were available to Mexican industry.

IEM feels that Westinghouse has been most cooperative in providing new technology needed. It undertakes little R&D on its own, believing that it is cheaper to obtain know-how under license from either West-inghouse or other foreign sources. Although most of the technology is obtained from Westinghouse, IEM has found that its bargaining position with other foreign firms has been strengthened through its association with Westinghouse. Extensive training support is provided to IEM engineers and technicians by Westinghouse in all elements of product design, process engineering, and manufacturing.

Certain trade-offs are evident in the IEM-Westinghouse joint venture in terms of the extent to which it achieves national technological objectives. While the Mexican partner obtains capital, training support, and internationally competitive, advanced know-how as well as considerable control over management decisions, it may, through the association with Westinghouse, have moved to a technological level beyond its absorptive capabilities. This will tend to slow down its own indigenous design/engineering development.

A third enterprise we shall consider under this category of Mexican-controlled joint ventures is Kimberly-Clark de Mexico, of which forty-three percent is owned by the Kimberly-Clark Corporation, a world-wide manufacturer of paper and nonwoven materials made from both cellulose and synthetic fibers—and fifty-seven percent by Mexican nationals. Kimberly-Clark (K-C) first entered the Mexican market in the early 1930s by exporting products through a local distributor. In 1955, it acquired substantial interest in a local paper manufacturer (La Aurora) and began producing select consumer products as well as printing and writing papers locally.

In 1962, Kimberly-Clark departed from the traditional pattern of MNC operations in Mexico by listing K-C de Mexico on the Bolsa, the Mexican stock exchange, and forty percent of the company's stock was sold to Mexican investors. According to K-C, this move proved to be a turning point for the company. Through their equity participation, some of the most successful businessmen in Mexico became interested in the business. Their advice was solicited and followed as how best to run a business in the country. Many of these individuals were asked to serve on the K-C de Mexico Board of Directors. One young man, Claudio Gonzalez, was selected to be the protege of the experienced Mexican board members. K-C attributes much of its subsequent success to the Mexican concern's strong management team built around Gonzalez and his strong Board. K-C de Mexico has grown in the past twenty years from a $2 million company to one that today does a volume of $135 million.

In 1973, before Mexicanization was required by law, and on the advice of Gonzalez and the K-C de Mexico Board of Directors, K-C sold its majority position of sixty percent down to forty-three percent. The K-C U.S. Board and the K-C de Mexico Board met regularly and frequently to discuss problems and mutual opportunities. Virtually all manufacturing know-how is transferred from the U.S. company, accompanied by extensive training.

K-C de Mexico differs from the cases cited in the next section in that, while it took the most convenient route to Mexicanize, through selling equity, Kimberly-Clark U.S. has also transferred effective management, marketing, and financial control to its Mexican board. The fact remains, however, that technological decisions and product dynamics remain with the parent company.

U.S.-CONTROLLED JOINT VENTURE

This section explores the experiences of foreign subsidiaries in Mexico which have complied with the national law on Mexicanization by yielding a majority equity position to Mexican nationals. Virtually all technological decisions and effective management and marketing are controlled by the parent corporation. This enterprise group can make a substantial contribution to the nation's balance-of-payments situation by bringing large amounts of capital and internationally competitive technology to the country for high-volume export manufacturing. At the same time, however, enterprises in this group offer little in terms of enhancing indigenous design/engineering capabilities. The firms we shall consider are Union Carbide Mexicana, S.A., and duPont Mexicana.

Union Carbide Corporation (U.C.C.) established a wholly-owned and controlled subsidiary in Mexico in 1964. One decade later, under pressure from the government, the corporation sold forty percent of its equity to Mexican nationals, retaining sixty percent ownership. It was soon clear that this move was not sufficient to obtain Mexican Government cooperation, and the company decided to Mexicanize. Union Carbide preferred to Mexicanize the subsidiary through a Trust Agreement whereby the shares are gradually and progressively sold to the public by a bank. This preference was based on a desire to maintain the value of its stock on the market and the fear that immediate Mexicanization would precipitate a flight of capital from the company. The Registry for Foreign Investment, however, rejected Union Carbide's application for a Trust Agreement and it was compelled to sell equity directly on the stock market. Today, fifty-one percent of Union Carbide Mexicana is owned by Mexican nationals, forty percent by the parent corporation and nine percent by others.

The company's fears for its capital structure did not materialize and

Union Carbide Mexicana (U.C.M.S.A.) is a successful enterprise with sales in 1976 of almost $80 million. The company's products are exported to twenty foreign markets, and its export sales increased by fifty percent in 1976. Its main product lines are chemicals and plastics; consumer items such as batteries; gas derived from air separation plants; and carbon products, e.g., graphite electrodes, projector carbons, and midget carbons. Local content of the firm's manufacturing is quite high, ranging from eighty-six percent in carbon products to 100 percent in phenolic resins and compounds.

Strong support is provided by the U.C.C. in a variety of areas such as technical assistance and service, supply of advanced technology and advice, for both existing operations and in the implementation of new projects and expansions. During 1976, more than 250 technicians from Union Carbide were assigned to U.C.M.S.A. to give training in manufacturing, marketing, and development of new products as well as assistance in the construction and start-up of two air-separation plants and an agricultural chemicals manufacturing facility.

The Union Carbide Corporation, from most indications, appears to have been assured that its Mexican partner respects the propriety of its know-how and is, therefore, prepared to release some of its most sophisticated technology. The Insecticides Formulating Plant in Apodaca, N.L., which began operations in April 1976, is evidence of this fact. Employing highly competitive technology, the plant completed the final integration of pesticides which were formerly imported. Design/engineering and technological capability of the U.C.M.S.A. engineers and technicians are, by the country's standards, extremely advanced, and they have demonstrated particular expertise in making significant adaptations in U.C.C. know-how in terms of cost savings and scale of operations. The Mexican company signed its first international technology transfer agreement in February of this year with a Colombian firm (Andercol) for the manufacture of phenolic compounds.

Union Carbide Mexicana is in the process of fulfilling all regulations and requirements of the new Law on Patents and Trademarks. It reports no objections from U.C.C. that the U.C.C. trademarks it has traditionally employed will be linked on all products with U.C.M.S.A.'s new marks. The Mexican company attributes a recent substantial boost in sales, especially in battery products, to its use of the trademark "El Pilon" (the cat) and a corresponding logo of a cat stamped on its products and containers. One slogan that has been especially successful is "El Pilon Eveready es el Pilon."

All parties to the Mexicanization of U.C.M.S.A. at present are satisfied with the arrangement. From the Mexican Government's point of view, foreign capital is under national control and the country continues to receive competitive manufacturing know-how in a priority sector to serve the national market and for export to earn foreign exchange. Union Carbide Mexicana continues to receive capital as well as technology and access to world markets through U.C.C.'s international marketing system. And, for the Union Carbide Corporation, Mexicanization was not so painful, except perhaps in being compelled to take a minority equity position. Effective management and financial control have actually been retained, though, through the composition of the Board of Directors. Under the by-laws of U.C.M.S.A., ownership of a certain percent of the company's stock enables the owner to place one member on the Board of Directors. As the fifty-one percent Mexican equity is spread among numerous Mexican nationals, the majority of the Board is selected by the Union Carbide Corporation.

From all indications, U.C.C. has not abused this right and has established a Board representing diverse and largely Mexican interests. U.C.M.S.A., in fact, points with pride at the composition of its Board for departing from the traditional practice of foreign subsidiaries in Mexico of appointing "paper boards."

Such arrangements for Mexicanization as carried out in Union Carbide's case take several long strides beyond the owned and controlled foreign subsidiary. They stop considerably short, though, of transferring real management, technological, financial, and marketing functions under national control. While experience is being acquired by nationals in performing these functions, ultimate responsibility has been retained by the foreign corporation.

DuPont Mexicana, S.A. represents another limited form of Mexicanization by a foreign corporation. DuPont's involvement in the Mexican market dates back to the 1920s when it acquired an explosives plant in the country and operated it as an owned and controlled subsidiary. It entered into its first joint venture in 1958 for the production of titanium oxide (paint base). The 1958 Law of Basic and Necessary Industry, requiring majority Mexican ownership of petrochemical enterprise operating in the country, forced duPont to take on local partners. The facility came on-stream in 1960.

In selecting national partners for the titanium oxide operation as well as for subsequent expansion and diversification, the duPont Company had two criteria in mind. First, it looked for investors who had accumulated substantial capital, and secondly, it sought non-industrial partners who would have no cause to meddle in management. Thus far, none of duPont's Mexican partners has developed substantive management expertise.

Approximately twelve companies compose the duPont Group in Mexico today, and in a majority of them, duPont holds a majority equity position. A partnership with PEMEX comes as close to joint management as any of duPont's Mexican concerns. Known as TEMSA (Tetraetilo de Mexico, S.A.), the operation manufactures high-volume industrial petrochemicals and is forty-nine percent owned by duPont and fifty-one percent owned by the state oil company. TEMSA employs internationally competitive manufacturing technology largely developed by duPont, and reinforced by PEMEX know-how. An important factor motivating duPont to accept the equity division is the fact that PEMEX enjoys a captive domestic market. The operation at the same time, however, is a source of tremendous pride to PEMEX, as it manufactures in the internationally competitive cost range.

U.S. chemical firms have been in a unique position to assist their Mexican partners in scaling down plant operations (at best, usually ten to fifteen percent of U.S. scale) to minimize the inevitable cost increase per unit of output. DuPont, for example, was able to redesign a plant originally built in the U.S. in the early 1920s by reducing the number of process steps, using more labor, and replacing certain less reliable mechanical control systems. In another case an earlier plant prototype originally built in France was redesigned to change chemical reaction procedures to conform to Mexican factor costs and scale requirements. A third case involved a polymer raw material used in extending optical quality plastic film; the process was redesigned based upon the "minimal, adequate" quality required for the Mexican market and in order to utilize much less costly, low-volume processing equipment in conjunction with an increased amount of low-wage Mexican labor.

DuPont's activities in the area of scaling down manufacturing operations to accommodate national factory availabilities make an invaluable contribution to the industrial sector of the Mexican economy. Rarely, however, do Mexican engineers participate in a central capacity in this task. This, in fact, is the situation for most functions performed by duPont Group companies. The Mexican economy gains by obtaining capital and know-how from duPont, but little is achieved toward enhancing indigenous design/engineering and technological capabilities.

CASE STUDY–FINANCIAL MECHANISMS

In the summer of 1979, the Mexican Government received a $5 million line of credit from the World Bank to finance loans to Mexican enterprises for the upgrading of industrial technology. This loan was a ground-breaking effort to provide funds direct to industrial enterprises to use as they saw fit to buy technical support services from either domestic or foreign firms. This represented an innovation in the institutional approach to advancing Mexico's technological absorptive and self-generating capabilities. Mexican authorities had previously used public funds largely to build up industrial research or related industrial technical support services. The line of credit was extended to FONEI (Fondo de Equipamiento Industrial), which is the financial arm of the Banco de Mexico responsible for funding manufacturing for export or exporting domestic manufacture that is nearly competitive with international costs. Specifically, the new fund provides for direct loans to Mexican enterprises to finance new or improved product or process development or investments in people, facilities, and equipment to carry out these activities.

As background to design of the new line of credit a survey of Mexican industrial enterprise was undertaken to obtain information on: (a) the sources of industrial technology; (b) the technical needs of these firms; and (c) projects that these firms would like to undertake.

The companies surveyed range from a fairly large division of an even larger conglomerate with sales over U.S.$280 million and employing several thousand people to small enterprise units with sales under U.S.$350,000 and employing fewer than 200 people. The products manufactured by surveyed firms range from spices and frozen citrus fruits to specialty steel products and equipment for oil rigs (see Figure III-1). Some firms produce a wide range of products, while others specialize in the production of a single line. The technical capabilities vary greatly among the enterprises surveyed—ranging from substantial research, development, and engineering capabilities, to firms with minimal capabilities to resolve technological adjustment problems.

The principal sources of industrial technology acquisition mentioned by surveyed firms were: (a) comprehensive licensing and purchase agreements with various foreign industrial firms; (b) assistance for both foreign and domestic engineers and technicians; (c) the training abroad of the company's Mexican technicians; and (d) in-house research, design, and engineering efforts. (See Figure III-1, column 3.)

The main needs for technical assistance that were cited by surveyed firms include: (a) new or improved product designs; (b) new or improved equipment and process design-engineering; and (c) improved quality control procedures. Several companies produce supplies for rapidly developing domestic industries and must meet the continually changing demands of their markets.

Proposed solutions for which the surveyed enterprises would presumably use the ITIF funding include: (a) the use of in-house design and engineering groups to develop new products and production processes; (b) the negotiation of technical service agreements with foreign industrial suppliers of operational technology; (c) technical information searches and training of Mexican technicians abroad; and (d) visits by foreign technical experts to advise on product-process-equipment design and engineering problems.

The cross-section of firms surveyed revealed an array of differences at the enterprise level in terms of in-house research, development, and engineering capabilities. Surveyed firms of different sizes and capabilities depended upon foreign sources to analyze and resolve technical problems in varying degrees. The proposed ITIF was designed to serve the following categories of Mexican firms:

- Firms that have at least a nucleus technical staff not only to diagnose problems, but to carry out segments of technical solutions and to find and negotiate for complementary foreign technical inputs of people, equipment, and information.

- Firms that still rely, to a substantial degree, upon outside sources to diagnose and resolve their technological adjustment problems, but are able to contract for such services from Mexican or foreign sources.

- Inventors or proposed new enterprise groups that have a technical innovation somewhere between the laboratory and commercial prototype stage and need funding to bring the innovation to a stage where it can be considered by commercial investment banks.

The following categories of company-funded activities were to be funded under the new line of credit:

- Research, design, or engineering projects involving adjustments in product or component design, new or improved production methods or materials processing, new or improved equipment design, experimentation with new industrial materials, or other related RD&E activities.

- Training of Mexican engineering or technical personnel abroad, including visits to industrial plants, research laboratories, or other industrial technical facilities, or for specialized training in applied research fields in foreign research institutes.

- Visits to Mexico by foreign technicians and engineers to advise on solutions to technical adjustment problems; to train research, design, or engineering personnel to find solutions to technical problems; or to provide other technical adjustment support services.

- Purchase of technical information (drawings and specifications for manufacturing equipment, materials processing, or product designs); quality control or testing equipment; or other tangible hardware needed in the technical adjustment process, including pilot plant construction.

- Technology audits and world market scanning services (for new product developments and equipment designs) of the type carried out by INFOTEC. FONEI may even suggest a technology audit in borderline cases involving firms with limited experience in diagnosing and resolving technological adjustment problems.

A simple and straightforward procedure was established to facilitate ITIF borrowing. The loan application review was to be limited to determining that: (a) the borrower was creditworthy; (b) the purposes for which the funds were to be used were categorically defined; and (c) the proposed use of funds was reasonably sound in terms of objectives and programmed effort. Projects were not to be reviewed for either commercial or economic benefit. Basic judgment on what to do, how to do it, and whether the effort was likely to result in commercial advantage rested with the firm, and not with FONEI.

It was essential to the successful implementation of the new line of credit that FONEI staff take an active role in making known to potential clients (previous borrowers and other firms known to be interested in technological upgrading) that funds are available and to explain to them the objectives and terms of these loans. In some cases, it was envisioned that it would be necessary to assist clients in formulating requests for funds and in negotiating with them appropriate categories and levels of funding. It was also anticipated that IMIT and INFOTEC, each with its unique network of contacts, could act as intermediaries in identifying potential clients in helping to prepare proposals. Both of the organizations had expressed an interest in performing these functions and felt that in many cases they could become involved in carrying out funded projects.

The proposed ITIF was viewed as a "structured experiment" requiring further adjustments to assure that the basic objectives of the

ITIF are carried out. Based upon the experience gained from proposal submissions and in negotiations with potential borrowers, it could be assumed that adjustments would be made in costs that would be covered and in percentages of project costs that FONEI would finance.

The survey of Mexican industry turned up a number of projects that involved an inordinate level of risk and uncertainty. This was particularly true of investors seeking funding of the first-stage laboratory prototype or the second-stage commercial prototype, including at times a pilot plant facility. (See Figure III-1, projects 5, 10, 11 and 13.) It was recommended therefore that FONEI and the Banco de Mexico explore where and how an additional line of credit could be placed with another financial institution that had the combined technical and commercial evaluation staff usually associated with venture capital companies in the United States or specialized merchant banks in Europe.

FOOTNOTES

[1]In 1977, the government reinstated certificates of tax rebates (known by the Spanish acronym CEDIS) for exports of manufactured and semi-manufactured goods which contain a minimum of thirty percent national content. Rebates on indirect taxes range from twenty to 100 percent, depending on the percentage of local content and volume of exportation. In addition, exporters have been exempted from a new surtax on gross profits, and they are due to receive tax rebates equivalent to 100 percent of the tax that would result from such profits.

[2]Based upon study carried out by RNTT in 1976.

[3]This is not an uncommon but a somewhat misguided attribution of blame to foreign enterprise, when, in fact, low economic performance is as much traceable to excessive protectionism and import substitution and misguided fiscal and monetary policies.

[4]See reference to analogous process design changes by duPont in its controlled subsidiaries, pages 93-94.

[5]Cydsa's negotiations with the U.S. firm Hercules for DMT technology broke down over the scale factor. Years later, and after the Mexican market had grown substantially, Hercules returned to Mexico.

LIST OF ABBREVIATIONS

CICIC	Scientific Research Development and Coordination Commission
CNIE	National Foreign Investment Commission
COMICYT	Inter-Institutional Scientific and Technological Commission
COMPLANCYT	National Planning and Technological Planning Commission
CONACYT	National Council for Science and Technology
FOGAIN	Guarantee and Development Fund for Small- and Medium-Sized Industry; Industrial Guarantee Fund
FOMEX	Fund for the Development of Manufactured Exports
FOMIN	National Fund for Industrial Development
FONATUR	National Tourism Development Fund
FONEI	Industrial Equipment Fund
FONEP	National Preinvestment Studies Fund
IEM	Electric Industry of Mexico
IIIE	Electric Industrial Research Institute
IMCE	Mexican Institute of Foreign Trade
IMCYC	Mexican Cement and Concrete Institute
IMIS	Mexican Steel Research Institute
IMIT	Mexican Technical Research Institute
IMP	Mexican Petroleum Institute
INFOTEC	Technical Information Trust Fund
INIC	National Institute of Scientific Research
ITIF	Industrial Technology Improvement Fund
LANFI	National Industrial Development Laboratories
NAFINSA	National Financiera, S.A.
PEMEX	Petroleos Mexicanos, S.A.
RNIE	National Foreign Investment Registry
RNTT	National Registry for the Transfer of Technology
SECOBI	Data Banks Consultancy Services
SIC	Ministry of Industry and Commerce
SOMEX	Mexican Society of Industrial Credit

CHAPTER IV
COLOMBIA*

INTRODUCTION

The developmental objectives of Colombia place strong emphasis upon continued economic growth and a more equitable income distribution. A basic strategy to realize these objectives is through enhanced efficiency and competition, to be achieved through the technological upgrading of Colombian industry. Another basic strategy is to intensify the exploitation of the country's mineral and energy resources. More equitable income distribution is to be achieved through purposeful efforts to further decentralize industrialization from the existing urban centers and to mount specific programs to increase income and employment among the rural and urban poor.

In the mineral and energy sector, American firms have encountered a rapidly changing operational environment. The new "associated agreements" (described later in the chapter) which have been negotiated with U.S. and other foreign enterprises, are symptomatic of the Government's determination to move in the direction of progressive managerial and technological command of the country's resources and downstream basic industries. The success of certain U.S. firms in accommodating the changing environment stands in contrast to U.S. firms that have insisted on doing business in the traditional ownership and control pattern, and, as a result, have been edged out of Colombia. Other business opportunities will be jeopardized if the United States fails to recognize the determination of the Colombian Government to develop its resource base in ways supportive of national development objectives.

THE ECONOMY AND TECHNOLOGY

Technology Factor in National Development

Colombia has reached a stage of social and economic development where substantial increases in productivity are needed in order to sustain economic growth. At the same time, unemployment problems and uneven income distribution necessitate substantial human and capital

---

*A list of abbreviations will be found at the end of the Chapter.

resource reallocation. Rural and urban poverty continue to be pressing problems. Colombian Government planners are fully cognizant of the need for a dual development strategy which increases productivity while redistributing income.

The plan to redistribute income consists in part of decentralizing small and medium-sized industries into rural areas, thereby creating employment opportunities and raising income levels. Special emphasis has been directed to development of the agribusiness sector. Through tax, interest and exchange rate policies and related monetary measures, government authorities hope to redirect previous policies, such as excessive import substitution, which have allocated resources inefficiently. Other redistributive programs include efforts to upgrade output in agricultural regions and plans to encourage the proliferation of labor-intensive industries.

Efforts to increase productivity are linked to the structural transformation of Colombia into an urban, industrial economy which is competitive in world markets. The financing of economic growth depends to a large degree upon exchange earnings from energy and mineral resources as well as the continued expansion of export of manufactured goods. One focal point of restructuring is the agribusiness sector with a view toward redesigning products and commodity processing to improve quality standards and efficiency for export markets. Growth of export industries involves in part the extensive upgrading of technological capabilities through use of various financial and technical support measures. Long-term programs include plans for the development of new mineral resources for export to strengthen Colombia's foreign exchange position.

State-owned enterprises are spearheading development of Colombia's coal, nickel, gas and petrochemicals industries, but the Colombian Government also is relying heavily upon the private sector to support expansion in these sectors. The latter will require economic incentives including favorable financial arrangements, to ensure an adequate flow of credit to the private sector, as well as augmenting the influx of private external capital. The development of technological absorptive capabilities and supply structures for the design and engineering of production systems is part of the long-term growth objectives of Colombian planning authorities.

Sector Priorities

Energy resources development is considered a leading link in development. The dual aim is to effectively explore for and exploit oil, coal, and gas resources and to retain managerial control in Colombian hands.

This also applies to future mineral development. State enterprises such as ECOPETROL (oil and gas) and CARBOCOL (coal) have been negotiating "associated agreements" with U.S. and other foreign firms to provide exploration, mining, and processing technologies. The main points of contention in the past over foreign involvement have been: (a) Colombian participation in resource management; (b) the sharing of technical data developed in connection with exploration operations; (c) the training of Colombians in the full range of technical-managerial tasks; and (d) price and profit-sharing formulae.

Colombia does not have the exchange reserve position to replace foreign investment in the mineral and energy resource area, and this has heretofore limited its bargaining position to obtain foreign technology and managerial support on its terms. In the case of nickel, where the ore benefication technology is relatively complex and the developmental costs relatively high, Colombia has had to yield majority equity position to foreign investors.

Another priority development area is the export sector in manufactured goods, involving mostly medium-to-smaller-sized Colombian firms. The main problem is technical upgrading to enter more competitive world markets, compared to the protected domestic markets in which most national firms have evolved. Present regulations governing technology imports in Colombia are part of the Andean Pact regime. The latter sets limits on what can be imported and on levels of payments, and it compounds the technological development problems faced by Colombian industrial enterprises. Foreign-owned firms bring technology with them and are able to bypass the payment restrictions that inhibit Colombian firms and thus place the latter at a competitively disadvantageous position. The larger Colombian-owned and managed enterprises are in a much stronger financial and technical position to develop or adapt product designs and adjust production methods to local needs and conditions than are smaller-size Colombian firms with more limited financial and managerial resources and capabilities. Smaller-sized Colombian-owned firms have difficulties both in diagnosing their technical problems and in effectively carrying out appropriate action.

A third priority area is raising employment and income levels among the rural and urban poor populations. The Government is particularly anxious to develop programs that raise productivity of low-income groups, and to assure maximum return of these gains to the poor. One possible approach is through the development of new small-scale enterprise firms and income-earning projects that integrate the two dimensions of productivity gains and income shares. Such programs require adapting to the needs and emerging capabilities of involved populations, appropriate training and technical assistance programs, and supporting institutional networks.

National Policies for Scientific and Technological Development

National science and technology policies and programs in support of economic growth and development have been influenced in part by the Andean Code,[1] whose broad objectives are to reduce technological dependence on foreign sources through restrictions on foreign private investment and the national control of foreign licensing agreements, and to develop indigenous technological acquisition and adaptation capabilities in support of national enterprise. The latter include the support and development of national laboratory facilities and an indigenous capital goods industry. Through the Andean Code, proposals have been made to create a central technology purchase agency supported by a regional science and technology information center. Other programs include the sponsorship of regional development projects, such as the processing of copper, the use of tropical forest resources, and various projects in the petrochemical industries.

Intervention in enterprise decisions is regarded as a necessary step toward national technological development. It is generally believed that the only way to deal with the adverse effects of uncontrolled foreign technology acquisition is through the systematic control of technology transfers as recommended under the Andean Pact Code. Among the criticisms levelled against industrial technology acquired from foreign sources is that it: (a) does little to resolve the problems of urban unemployment; (b) tends to be capital-wasting as measured by the capital costs per job generated; (c) contributes to further concentration of economic power in terms of the size of enterprise units and of income distribution efforts; and (d) fails to minimize use of imported materials.

TECHNOLOGY SUPPORT STRUCTURES AND MECHANICS

Government Sector

Principal government agencies impacting on the technology component in national development are: (a) the National Planning Department within the Ministry of Planning whose Private Investment Division screens the technology component of foreign investment proposals; (b) the Exchange Control Office which evaluates foreign technical assistance contracts; (c) the Global Licenses Committee of the International Trade Institute (INCOMEX) which evaluates applications to import machinery and equipment; and (d) the Royalties Committee which screens foreign licensing contracts. Varied attempts have been made to channel these control mechanisms into a more comprehensive set of national policies and programs.

The Private Investment Division of the National Planning Department screens the technology component of foreign investment proposals, and the Royalties Committee screens foreign licensing contracts. These two agencies coordinate their efforts with a view toward improving the country's bargaining position with respect to foreign suppliers of industrial technology. Criteria used for evaluation are: (a) effect on the balance-of-payments; (b) increase in employment; (c) productivity of foreign exchange spent in the project; and (d) use of internal resources.

The Exchange Control Office approves foreign technical assistance contracts, and the Global Licenses Committee (INCOMEX) is in charge of approvals for imported machinery and equipment. It evaluates applications according to their congruence with the National Development Plan, taking into consideration: (a) the protective structure; (b) balance-of-payment effects; and (c) tax policy.

COLCIENCIAS (Colombian National Fund for Scientific Research and Special Projects) is charged with developing national policies for science and technology in support of economic development. In attempting to fortify the country's autonomous capacity for technical innovation, COLCIENCIAS has advocated programs to stimulate demand for science and technology capabilities in Colombia through: (a) government purchase of capital goods; (b) technical information systems for purchasers of industrial technology; and (c) preferred treatment in allocating research, engineering and other technical support services.

COLCIENCIAS has favored policies to: (a) prohibit the import of large-scale equipment (to avoid further concentration of industry); and (b) disaggregate imported technology packages, with a view towards maximizing procurement of technology components from national sources. They have been in favor of some form of subsidy or incentive to encourage industrial enterprises to undertake technical research projects (one possibility being the Peruvian system of levying a two percent tax on all firms to fund such activities). They also have recommended that special funding be provided for "high-risk" industrial projects in national priority areas, such as food and nutrition and minerals and energy resource development.

Two other groups working in close collaboration with COLCI-ENCIAS are IIT (Institute for Technology Investigations) and SENA (National Training Institute). IIT conducts research on technology projects; SENA is in charge of upgrading technical and managerial expertise in Colombia and of forging the link between the traditional and modern sectors of the economy by encouraging the spread of efficient industrial practice.

SENA has had an important role in advancing technical capabilities at the enterprise level. Their programs are designed to improve or advance production systems either through product design, redesign of production lines or improved efficiency of manufactured technology and processing of intermediate materials. SENA maintains a network of seventeen field offices as training and extension service centers. Its funds (over $60 million annually) are derived from a two percent tax on all wages. Their programs are aimed at achieving technological development in Colombia through industrial training and consulting services in support of rural and urban small-scale industrial enterprises.

SENA's specific objectives are: (a) to form a Colombian professional corps; (b) to institute programs to assist small-scale rural and urban industries in order to benefit the poorest segments of the population; (c) to prepare individuals for management positions; and (d) to be a source of information for small-scale industry concerning all aspects of business management.

SENA could extend its present industrial training and consulting services to cover technological adjustment at the small enterprise level and in rural industrial development to include the following:

1. Training in new equipment or new process techniques coupled with learning programs for small shop equipment.

2. A diagnostic service to include the appraisal of product designs and production techniques to advance productivity and market competitiveness.

3. Diagnosis and appraisal of additional SENA-sponsored support networks to: (a) design technology packages for small-scale plants in the agribusiness field; and (b) expand market opportunities through domestic and international subcontracting systems.

The Financial Community

Until recently, the financial community in Colombia has had a relatively minor role in supporting the advancement of technology at the enterprise level or in the economy at large. About two years ago, the Colombian Government initiated an experimental program through funds borrowed from the World Bank and channeled through the central bank (Banco de la Republica) to the private *financieras* for direct lending to private enterprises. (See below, Technology Sources and Needs.)

Business Enterprise

Colombian enterprise may be classified into four groups: public enterprise; large-scale, foreign-managed firms; large-scale, Colombian-managed firms; and medium-to-small, Colombian-managed entities. Based on the field work in Colombia, including the case materials (see below), an analysis and evaluation was made of enterprise capabilities to manage technology components ranging from planning the technology component of production systems to the utilization of acquired technology (see Figure IV-1).

The public enterprise sector consists of state-owned groups such as ECOPETROL (oil), CARBOCOL (coal), and ECONIQUEL (nickel), which are described in the case studies. Capabilities to plan and control the technology component of industrial systems which are being developed in the public enterprise sector under "associated agreements" are described in that section. Certain public enterprises are now attempting to develop indigenous design and engineering capabilities associated with their operational responsibilities.

There is a fairly well established private enterprise community in the town-centered areas of Cali and Medellin—where firms such as Coltejer (textiles) and Carvejal (printing) trace back to the turn of the century. Large Colombian-managed enterprises of more recent origin (such as Yidi Zipper) have developed very substantial capabilities to plan and implement the technology component. International contacts, including attendance at industrial fairs, assist larger firms in their technological acquisitions activities and in development of technical manpower.

Foreign-managed firms generally derive the technology component from the U.S. parent—although there are significant exceptions such as Carton de Colombia (a diversified paper product company owned by Container Corporation of America), which developed indigenous

FIGURE IV-1. EVALUATION OF ENTERPRISE CAPABILITIES IN
MOBILIZING TECHNOLOGY COMPONENTS (COLOMBIA)

FUNCTIONAL TASKS	PUBLIC ENTERPRISE – ECOPETROL – ECONIQUEL – CARBOCOL	PRIVATE ENTERPRISE		
		LARGE-SCALE FIRMS (Foreign Managed)	LARGE-SCALE FIRMS (Colombian Managed)	MEDIUM-TO-SMALL FIRMS (Colombian Managed)
PLANNING • Policy Coordination • Project Formulation	Capabilities to plan and control technology component greatly improved in recent years.	Most strategic decisions involving planning of technology component handled by foreign partner.	Gradually expanding capabilities to plan and control technology component of production systems.	Capabilities limited to skill and experience of manager-owner.
GENERATING • Research • Development • Design Engineering	Now attempting to develop in-house capabilities to carry out RD&E projects in connection with operational responsibilities.	Some firms such as Carton de Colombia and SIMESA have taken substantial initiative in developing operational technology.	A small number of firms undertake limited range of RD&E on product design adjustments and process design.	Generally incapable of undertaking efforts on their own—limited support from small groups such as FICITEC.
SEARCHING • Technical Information • Licensing Sources	Gradually developing capabilities to search for alternative technology sources.	Depends in large part upon foreign partner for technology.	Many have developed networks of contacts abroad with equipment and material suppliers and their attendance at international industrial fairs.	Limited capabilities to seek out technology appropriate to scale and other production requirements.

NEGOTIATING • Technology Acquisition	Gradually developing astuteness and skill in negotiating for technology from foreign sources.	(See above.)	Larger firms have developed astuteness and skill in negotiating for technology through foreign contacts.	Limited in-house capabilities—largely dependent upon equipment and materials suppliers that visit Colombia.
SUPPORTING • Standards • Quality Control • Extension Services	Substantial capabilities derived in part from foreign technology partners.	Often rely on foreign technicians for technical assistance.	Most firms have substantial quality control and other technical support capabilities.	Rely in part on equipment and materials suppliers for technical support services. Some support from groups such as FICITEC.
TRAINING • Professional • Managerial • Technicians	Programs to develop top managers and technicians part of new Associated Agreements.	Have substantial in-house capabilities obtained in large part from foreign parent.	Firms often able to arrange for technical training through foreign contacts.	Limited in-house capabilities. Receive some training from SENA (National Training Institute).
USING • Installation • Operation • Maintenance	Substantial capabilities derived in part from foreign affiliates who supply technology, equipment and materials.	Substantial capabilities derived in large part from foreign parent.	Generally have substantial in-house capabilities to operate physical plant.	Capabilities limited to skill and training of owner-managers.

technology for processing tropical hardwoods and has become a highly self-sufficient company technologically.

It is the small-to-medium enterprises that tend to be highly dependent on foreign equipment and industrial materials suppliers for industrial know-how. These are generally incapable of undertaking technical adjustment tasks (RD&E), and have limited search and negotiating capabilities. Small firms rely on government agencies such as SENA for technical training and on private organizations such as FICITEC for technical support services.

Technology Sources and Needs

Significant insights on how and where Colombian firms acquired their manufacturing know-how and related technical capabilities to further adapt or design products and production processes were obtained from a mini-survey carried out by the author in the spring of 1975. The survey was carried out in connection with an experimental line of credit extended by the World Bank to local industrial investment banks (*financieras*) for loans to Colombian enterprises to finance technology upgrading efforts.[2] The results of this survey are summarized in Figure IV-2.

The sixteen firms surveyed were located largely in Medellin, Cali and Barranquilla, and represented a broad range of industrial subsectors, company sizes and stages of commercial and technical development. Virtually all of the companies interviewed said they had benefitted from foreign technology sources. Colombian firms that were not subsidiaries of foreign companies relied primarily on foreign licensing sources and foreign equipment suppliers for technological support. Many firms employed foreign technical managers and/or technical advisors at one time or another, sometimes for extended periods. Most Colombian firms surveyed considered it essential to maintain linkages to foreign technology sources, rather than to rely upon indigenous research and development. The reason for this was that it takes considerable time and resources to develop new or improved products or processes.

As commercial opportunities to supply domestic markets have been exhausted, Colombian firms began to turn to export markets and faced intensified competition at home and abroad. This has led to the need for technological upgrading of product designs and production techniques, and most of the firms visited expressed an interest in financing to assist them in this regard.

Some of the more successful firms had initiated specific programs to

FIGURE IV-2. SURVEY OF COLOMBIAN ENTERPRISE TECHNOLOGY SOURCES AND NEEDS

FIRM (INDUSTRY)	COMMERCIAL ACTIVITIES	FOREIGN SOURCES OF TECHNOLOGY	TECHNOLOGICAL CHARACTERISTICS AND NEEDS
1. Carvajal (Graphic Arts)	Firm produces a wide range of printed materials—all potentially competitive in international markets. Annual sales over U.S. $44 million, of which U.S. $7 million (15%) is exported.	Technical managers from Germany and other European countries, for short-term run-in and trouble-shooting. Technicians trained abroad with equipment suppliers and licensors. Have used IESC (Int'l Exec. Service Corps) technicians for quality control and introduction of new product lines.	Carvajal has had difficulties with royalty payments to foreign technology sources, and over import permits for new rotary presses, needed to retain competitive position. Firm wishes to purchase licenses, and to conduct research and engineering of new product lines and production techniques.
2. Carton de Colombia (Pulp and Paper)	Highly integrated operation from forest management through pulp and paper and the manufacture of various packaging materials. Annual sales U.S. $70 million of which U.S. $16 million (23%) is exported.	Sixty-five percent owned and controlled subsidiary of Container Corporation of America. All American managers replaced by Colombians in 1950. Most R&D conducted jointly with local researchers and foreign technicians.	Firm has developed unique technology to process domestically available hardwoods from mixed tropical forests. Reforestation program based on genetic adaptation of softwoods transplanted from elsewhere. Need for coöperative ventures with public authorities to develop product lines and production techniques.
3. Casa Schaps (Trading Company)	Firm processes and exports tobacco (to North Africa), pre-cut lumber (to Europe and U.S.), and manufacturers brushes for local market. The latter account for only 5% of sales, but 40% of profits. Annual sales about U.S. $5 million.	Bought out tobacco curing and packing operation from U.S. firm. Kiln drying techniques for lumber from equipment suppliers in UK, tungstein-tip treatment for saws from German supplier. Brush manufacturing techniques from supplier of automatic sawing machines in Germany. Contacts with equipment/process suppliers by visits to factories abroad. Have used IESC experts for machine layout and technical operations.	Has utilized standard technologies, but would like to observe foreign technology sources in brush manufacturing and cigar making fields to expand product lines and to fund visits by foreign technicians to improve sawmill practices.

FIGURE IV-2—CONTINUED

4. Coolecheria (Dairy Product)	Dairy product firm with annual sales about U.S. $1.8 million.	Most of technology from process equipment suppliers: milk powder (U.S.), pasteurizers (UK), bottle cappers (UK), and new pasteurizer (E. Germany). Foreign technicians from IESC to advise on butter processing conveyor systems, cost reduction, and improved quality control procedure.	When Nestle-subsidiary (CICOLAC) recently installed new electronic milk processing plant, Coolecheria bought out their old equipment. Firm operates and is able to compete with more modern facilities only a few months a year—when milk is available and in high demand season. Would like to expand milk powder production and to establish office cream plant. The company could benefit from visits from foreign technicians and to foreign plants and licensing/equipment sources in connection with ice cream/milk powder plant expansion.
5. Duncan Industrial (Metal Working)	Firm manufactures variety of metal fasteners (nickel, zinc, bronze, copper, black oxide). Annual sales under U.S. $500,000, of which U.S. $60,000 (15%) is exported.	Licensing agreement with U.S. firm (Plymouth Cordage). Director is a U.S.-trained mechanical engineer with U.S. experience in tool and die-making, also toured factories in France (Newey Bros.).	U.S. engineer has designed and engineered many of the items manufactured (or adapted foreign prototype), and is now developing an electronic safety lock—for which he sees expanding domestic and foreign market. Standard technology, but expresses need for foreign visits; needs funds for lump sum payment of newly negotiated licensing agreements, and for design and engineering of new product line.
6. Everfit (Textiles)	Manufacturer of textiles and men's apparel. Integrated operation from spinning machines to produce fibers through	Equipment suppliers (spinning machines fabric sizing and finishing, and vat dyeing) from Germany, Switzerland, Italy, UK, and U.S. Continuing visits to textile factories in Switzerland, Germany	Firm has utilized traditional manufacturing techniques from foreign sources; expresses need to borrow money to send technicians abroad to learn new fabric processing techniques.

FIGURE IV-2—CONTINUED

	textile weaving and dyeing and clothing manufacture. Annual sales U.S. $7 million, of which nearly U.S. $3 million is exported, largely to U.S. market as ready-made suits under Pierre Cardin label.	and UK. Materials suppliers (chemical dyes and fabric adhesives (another important source of technology. Attend international fairs on textile machines for new ideas and processing techniques. Two-year contracts with European technicians since 1965 to set up machine maintenance systems.	
7. FUNDENTE (Heavy Mechanical Equipment)	Manufactures components for heavy mechanical equipment (such as steel foundries and sugar refineries) in both ferrous and non-ferrous metals such as bronze.	Arranged for short-term visit of Japanese industrial technician to advise them on moving into lighter industrial components for automotive industry. Contact made through Corporation Financiera del Valle (Cali), who in turn contacted the Industrial Development Bank of Japan, one of their stockholders. JDBJ in turn contacted a leading automotive parts manufacturer, Riken, who in turn agreed to send a technician to advise FUNDENTE.	Traditional line of technology, for additional visits by foreign technicians to advise on expansion of product line, and for visits abroad to negotiate new licensing arrangements.
8. Industries Emilio Yidi e Hijos (Zippers)	Zipper manufacturing firm. Annual sales U.S. $2.7 million of which approximately 25% (U.S. $670,000) is exported, mostly to Andean Group countries. Firm manufactures 15,000 varieties of	Two of the brothers who own the factory spent six months in the U.S. learning tool and die making. At first, firm produced replacement tooling and parts for purchased machines; now they manufacture their own. Yidi has reduced standard nine-step zipper manufacturing procedure to three steps. Visits to foreign zipper manufacturers and	Stamping machines digest rolls of fabric and metal and turn out continuous finished elements of programmed teeth size and zipper length. Heart of operation is tool and die making for the zipper style variations. Much of zipper semi-automated equipment is designed by Yidi, which expresses no current technological needs.

FIGURE IV-2—CONTINUED

zippers.		equipment suppliers have helped maintain technological parity with world competition. Have used IESC experts to improve cost and quality control, mechanical maintenance procedures, and plant layout.	Relatively standard technology; expressed need to finance visits of foreign technical advisers to Colombia and to fund an R&D design team in plastic products design and production engineering (particularly improved quality control).
9. IMUSA-Industries Metalurgicas Unidas (Aluminum and Plastic)	Firm manufactures aluminum and plastic houseware goods. Annual sales about U.S. $2.8 million, exports insignificant. About 20 percent of output is industrial components.	German technical director since 1935 with specialty in aluminum extrusions. Spanish technician 1941-45 on plastic manufacture. License from American Can Company (U.S.) terminated by Colombian Government as unwarranted after 20 years. Another license from U.S. company still operative for electric frying pans. Production technology also derived from equipment suppliers in France, Germany and U.S. Technician went to Austria for three months training in plastic manufacturing techniques.	
10. Industria Nacional de Repuestos (Automotive Parts)	Automotive parts (shock absorbers, etc.). Annual sales U.S. $3.3 million. Exports negligible (less than U.S. $30,000). About 70% sales for replacement parts, with the remainder to auto assembly industries as original equipment.	Licensing agreements with three or four U.S. firms, who provide complete technology package.	This firm produces in protected seller's market and is technologically dependent upon foreign licensing sources. Not much interest in moving into more competitive foreign market, for which a higher degree of technological initiative and self-reliance would be necessary.

FIGURE IV-2–CONTINUED

			Standard technology; would like to expand laboratory quality control and materials testing and to design new types of hydrants, cultivators, and heavy duty harrows.
11. Ingersoll-Apolo (Agricultural Implement)	Agricultural implement firm. Also manufactures pumping and hydrant equipment, spring brackets and brake drums. Annual sales about U.S. $6 million, of which about one-third (U.S. $2 million) is exported.	Licenses obtained some 15 years ago for harrows (U.S.), plows (UK) and valves (U.S.). More recently, licenses obtained for rock crushers (Allis-Chambers, U.S.) and brake drums (Chrysler, U.S.). Borg-Warner provides technology for clutches and plow discs under joint venture arrangement. Now negotiating license with German firm for new type of flexible hose valve connections with Massey-Ferguson to manufacture grain harvesters for Andean market. Segments of technology from equipment suppliers—foundry built in 1963. Mechanite (U.S.); more recently electric furnaces supplied by Braun-Boveri (Swiss) for auto parts foundry work. Have used IESC experts on foundry techniques.	
12. Loceria Colombiana (Porcelain)	Firm manufactures moderately priced line of porcelain dinnerware. Annual sales average about U.S. $5.5 million; about 5% (U.S. $180,000) exported to Puerto Rico. Protection in Colombia market close to 100%.	Product design and manufacturing know-how under license from U.S. firm dating back to 1960 (since terminated by Colombian Government after running ten years). Technical managers have visited porcelain factories in Germany, U.S., Argentina and Brazil. Portion of know-how from equipment suppliers of furnaces, mixers, compressors, and instrument controls in Germany, Switzerland and U.S. Have used IESC technical advisers on furnace operations, preparation of porcelain clays, and quality control procedures.	Standard manufacturing techniques; would like to explore technology sources in Italy and Germany for improved design and better dye materials for decorating and would like to purchase new equipment for improved quality control.

FIGURE IV-2—CONTINUED

13. Compania Pintuco (Chemicals and Metals)	Firm manufactures a range of chemical and metal products, including plasticizers, inks, paints, tin-plated cans, and mixing tanks. Annual sales about U.S. $23 million.	Know-how in chemicals field originally from Grace and Company, followed by a 10-15 year period without foreign licenses. Two year contract with UK firm for ink-making technology. Technicians sent abroad one to two months for training.	Standard technology mostly from foreign sources, but wants funds for laboratory equipment to analyze chemical products on market, so they can design their own versions.
14. RICA (Meat)	Firm manufactures meat products for Colombian market.	German technicians on sausage manufacture for one year; Swiss technician on meat products for over three years. Short-term specialists from U.S. consultant firm (International Food Engineering) on vacuum packing techniques, return and exchange systems for distributors, etc. Technical assistance from U.S. equipment and materials suppliers (Union Carbide).	Standard technology; firm is interested in exploring Caribbean export market and in meeting technical upgrading requirements. Could use funds to pay for technical advisers and for visits to new sources of upgraded technology.
15. SIMESA Siderurgica de Medellin (Foundry and Rolling Mill)	Foundry and rolling mill which fabricates steel billets, angles and shapes including tubes, rods, wire, plate and angles. Annual sales just over U.S. $14 million, of which about U.S. $1.3 million is exported.	Contract with Brazilian (Sao Paulo) steel foundry to help select equipment and train technicians. Construction steel extrusion technology from U.S. firm since 1960. Negotiating license with ARMCO Steel (Canada) for alloy steels to be supplied to Andean market.	Have developed own technology for chrome-carbon steel balls used in cement manufacture. Would like to expand into specialized low-carbon and alloy steels for Colombian and Andean markets, and to fund design and engineering teams to develop new steel products.

FIGURE IV-2–CONTINUED

16. UNIAL— Union Industrial y Astilleros (Heavy Industrial Equipment)	Manufactures a varied line of heavy mechanical equipment, including boilers, fishing and other commercial vessels, food processing equipment, and hydroelectric power dam gates.	Licenses from foreign equipment manufacturers: bottling (U.S.), power-system gates (France and Spain), and commercial vessels (Canada). Have used IESC advisers to improve welding techniques in vessel reactors. Some technology derived as subcontractors (to Allis-Chambers on clinkers for cement plants). Colombian-trained level architects used to develop designs for catamarans and other commercial vessels.	Joint venture with Canadian firm to design and engineer complementary line of fishing and other commercial vessels.

maintain awareness of technological alternatives and new process development through visits to international trade fairs and foreign factories
and by sending technicians abroad for training. In addition, they had
adopted an aggressive attitude towards diversifying licensing partners,
and equipment and raw material suppliers, and hiring foreign technical
advice. In contrast, other firms seemed content to rely for extended
periods on some packaged technology acquired from a foreign licensor
which enabled them to supply the protected national market profit-
ably. As for technological deficiencies, companies indicated they could
use these funds in three major ways: (a) to hire foreign technicians or
train technicians abroad to improve the efficiency of existing production processing; (b) to conduct research and development into new or
improved products and processes; and (c) to obtain medium-term financing to improve the bargaining position of the firm in acquiring
licenses to utilize new production processes. (See summary Figure
IV-2.)

CASE STUDIES—U.S.-COLOMBIAN
ENTERPRISE RELATIONS

Beginning in the early 1970s, the Colombian authorities began
focusing attention on the more effective management of the country's
energy and mineral resources—following in part the examples set by
Mexico and Venezuela. The two cases cited in this chapter relate to the
exploitation of Colombian hydrocarbon and nickel resources. They
describe the new "associated agreements" that Colombia has negotiated
with U.S. firms and which are aimed at striking a better balance between serving the country's long-term economic and technological development needs and continuing to attract foreign commercial interests.

ECOPETROL (Energy Resources)

ECOPETROL is the state enterprise charged with the responsibility
to find, obtain, and utilize non-renewable resources in the energy field.
It operates under several constraints, including the fact that Colombia's
financial resources are limited and neither ECOPETROL nor the
country at large have the technical capabilities to take the full risk of
exploring for oil. ECOPETROL is attempting to develop an expanding
level of self-sufficiency for its exploration teams, using foreign firms for
technical support activities such as geophysical services and seismographic analyses of data obtained in the field and later processed by

computer technology. Several American firms are under subcontract to process field data for ECOPETROL. A group of these computer analysis firms have offered to form a joint company to provide the services, but the Colombians prefer the flexibility of contracting for them as needed.

ECOPETROL manages its own operational teams in a wide range of activities, but in certain areas such as offshore drilling, they hire specialists in the United States and elsewhere. Contracting foreign technicians, as such, is not acceptable to Colombian labor interests, so contracts are negotiated with service companies to do specified work in Colombia with support facilities in the United States. Turnkey contracts are used with foreign companies which carry out specified tasks and are reimbursed on a performance basis—often at their own expense and risk in initial stages. Under these arrangements, Colombian personnel are often sent to service centers abroad for training to keep them up-to-date on technology and operational techniques. As for the sale of oil products, ECOPETROL is able to develop and manage the required infrastructure and to have necessary access to international marketing outlets.

ECOPETROL recognizes that there is considerable risk and uncertainty in the area of oil exploration and is not ready to go it alone. It realizes that in seismographic techniques, the technology is advancing rapidly and that computer analysis particularly is changing every day. It recognizes that the uncertainty of finding oil is much too high and that Colombian technical capabilities at this time are very modest. ECOPETROL has negotiated associated exploration agreements with American, Brazilian, French, and Roumanian groups. American firms are generally favored, because of their access to advanced technology. Service companies supporting ECOPETROL's own field exploration teams are all American. European firms are at a disadvantage technologically, and they are generally unwilling to risk expenditures on field exploration activities.

ECOPETROL has had approximately four years' experience with associated contract agreements, and it is now extending this experience to the exploitation of coal and gas resources. It entered into a joint venture with another Colombian Government agency, IFI (Instituto de Fomento Industrial), to create a new state enterprise, CARBOCOL, to develop Colombia's coal and gas resources. Several U.S. companies have expressed interest in purchasing natural gas derivatives from Colombia. One possibility is gas-derived chemicals such as ammonia-urea. The difficulty has been that the world market for urea products has been erratic and commercial interests in Colombia have not been willing to pay more than one-fourth of the world price for natural gas. As a result, the gas will be used domestically at a subsidized price, as it is in the case of gasoline, which sells well below international prices. Another problem in developing natural gas resources is that high volumes of utilization and production are required in order to amortize the high investment cost normally associated with the processing of natural gas. The Colombians are exploring a low-volume technology available in Spain. The Spanish system has a processing plant on board an ocean-going vessel, which can be anchored offshore to process the gas delivered through a pipeline, and then moved on to other processing sites.

ECOPETROL's associated contract agreements are based upon certain principles and developmental objectives, stemming from the fact that ECOPETROL is a state enterprise and must consider the public interest. For example, ECOPETROL often has imported petroleum at considerably higher prices than it is sold domestically, and it had to absorb the losses implicit in subsidies to local consumption of natural gas.

Colombian authorities are interested in maintaining their good reputation for adherence to contract agreements, but they have insisted on certain terms and conditions. They have reserved the right to renegotiate contracts periodically (usually every five years), and they also have insisted that foreign firms share technical information in adjacent exploration areas and that these foreign firms reciprocally have access to exploration information on areas adjacent to their exploration sites.

ECOPETROL has issued associated contract requests to some seventeen international firms, including up to nine U.S. companies. A major agreement has been signed with a subsidiary of the Exxon Corporation, Intercol Resources. ECOPETROL intends to retain full control over exploration rights for energy and mineral resources. It is also interested in applying the petroleum scheme to other energy and mineral resources including copper, uranium, and other metals.

These joint venture agreements have a life of thirty-one years. Exploration is limited to the first six years. The agreement expires at the end of this initial exploration period if no exploitable oil reserve is discovered. Costs incurred in the siesmic survey and the well drilling are assumed by the foreign company which recoups its expenses only if oil is found. Once these costs have been recouped, the company enters into an income-sharing agreement with ECOPETROL for a limited period. Even if the reserves have not been exhausted by the end of this period, Colombia receives complete ownership rights and control over the concession.

For a period of up to twenty-five years after the six-year exploration period, the foreign firm is entitled to recoup its initial investment which it has assumed alone and to share in the profits from the wells. The foreign firm is required to drill one well within the first year of the joint venture agreement and successive new wells every nine months thereafter until the six-year period is expired.

Once well operations have started, ECOPETROL and the foreign company create a joint account against which all costs of operations are charged. Until the foreign firm has recovered all its initial exploration costs, the share of output is divided two-thirds in favor of the foreign firm and one-third in favor of ECOPETROL. After this, output is divided on a fifty-fifty basis. Both companies take their percentages after a seventeen percent royalty is paid to the Colombian Government.

Each of the joint venturers can market its own share of petroleum or they can set up a joint facility to market this output. But the joint venture is under a restriction requiring it to fulfill domestic needs before exporting. If one of the parties is unable to assume its rights, the other party automatically assumes these rights and the associated profits. If the foreign firm wants to sell its assets in the joint venture, ECOPETROL has the right of first refusal.

All technical data developed during the exploration and development stage of the operation belong to both companies. In addition, although the agreement does not require the training of Colombian personnel, under Colombian law, a certain percentage of the employees must be Colombian.

Peabody (Coal)

Four years ago, Peabody Coal Co., a division of Kennecott Copper, was invited to enter negotiations with an agency of the Colombian Government, IFI (Instituto de Fomento Industrial), for the development of its coal reserves in the southeast region known as Cerrojon. The project was to involve exploration, mining and related infrastructural development, and international marketing. Peabody commenced its exploration on the basis of a letter of intent leaving numerous details on a final contract to be worked out at a later date. As of December 1976, no final agreement had been reached.

The extensive block for which Peabody has been negotiating represents one-third of the coal field. This subdivision is estimated to contain reserves of approximately 300 million tons of coal of which ninety million are known to be mineable. The coal is utility grade, low sulphur and has been approved for use in the U.S. by the Environmental Protection Agency.

The project has had numerous developmental problems. According to Peabody and representatives of an international agency, the Government of Colombia has created difficulties by allowing competition to develop among government agencies concerned with the Peabody negotiations. The total concession is controlled by IFI, ECOPETROL and CARBOCOL, which have conflicting interests. This joint control has meant that Peabody and other bidders have been obliged to meet requirements of all three agencies. Peabody claims that it has been prevented from developing a commercially viable scale of operation because of excessive regulations, such as demands for infrastructural development. Further difficulties have emerged from local land owners and political groups with whom Peabody has been obliged to make certain agreements.

The concession was subsequently allocated to several companies, which has further limited: (a) the size of the respective mines; (b) the financial viability of any one project; and (c) the possible types of mining operations in which any one firm may engage. Peabody claims that the concessions have been arbitrarily set out, and that the above factors have limited the amount of financial resources that Peabody is able to put into this project. Nevertheless, Peabody has invested several millions of dollars in exploration, but still has not negotiated a final contract. Peabody's expenditures have covered construction of a permanent camp for workers and associated exploration and assay work, most of which has been undertaken by U.S.-trained Colombian engineers.

Peabody is seeking to finance the project on the basis of long-term contracts with an end-user. A Florida utility has agreed to a thirty-year supply contract, if the project goes ahead. It would be difficult to get financing, even from the World Bank, without such a long-term agreement based upon a stabilized market price.

Substantial financing is needed particularly because of the demands for infrastructural development by IFI, which is interested in the development of a sophisticated, heavy-use rail facility, linked to port facilities, for use by the Peabody concession as well as neighboring concessions and industries. Peabody has agreed to build a broad-gauge line with a third rail for the narrow-gauge Colombian trains. This would provide minimal facilities, but it is not acceptable to IFI.

Peabody maintains that the limited mine concession for which it is negotiating cannot support the cost of a major rail system. According to Peabody, Exxon, which has been granted a neighboring concession, has also been asked to develop a rail system. CARBOCOL has asked Peabody to form a joint venture with Exxon. Peabody claims this indicates that Exxon's larger concession will also have difficulty in supporting this type of project.

There is further disagreement among all parties about whether division of the concession affects the type of mine operated and the valuation of the coal. Exxon and Colombian officials claim that if Peabody uses techniques other than surface mining, many more reserves will be recovered. Peabody will only undertake surface mining until it determines whether other types of mining will be financially practical. With regard to coal valuation, Peabody is assessing coal value on the basis of all related costs, in contrast to Exxon which has perhaps overestimated projected returns because of determination of coal value in terms of BTU oil equivalent, which greatly increases value. Further complications on pricing have emerged because of an inflated world price of coal at the time of negotiations, which is no longer tenable and which would now decrease the value of operations.

Because of disagreement about the actual recoverable reserves and the coal's value, IFI and Peabody have been unable to go beyond their agreement in principle to establish a joint venture trading and a separate mining company. The latter would be divided between IFI and CARBOCOL, with a minority equity position in the hands of Peabody. The government agencies would receive a majority of the dividends and would tax the entity at the full corporate rate.

The international trading company, as envisioned by IFI, would divide international sales efforts with Peabody. According to Peabody such an arrangement is not viable. First, there is inadequate proven mineable coal in the allocated block to justify the establishment of an international trading operation with a network of foreign offices as conceived by IFI. Second, shipping costs to distant markets cannot be absorbed in the price of this grade coal if it is to remain competitive. Third, as noted, Peabody does not believe it can finance the project without a long-term contract which would utilize virtually all production.

Exxon/Peabody (Oil-Coal)

Exxon has been involved in Colombia for several years. It has now sold off its refinery operations, but maintains a management services contract with the Colombian Government. Exxon believes that the Colombian Government has a deep and lasting respect for contracts and this ranges from the old concession agreements to the new associated contracts. The Colombians recognize that they need the financial resources to fund their operations and the training of technical personnel for future management and development of the country's resources. The new agreements covering oil and coal resource development con-

tain provisions for: (a) shared management of the joint venture consisting of three ECOPETROL and three Exxon executives; (b) sharing
technical information on all exploration operations; (c) use of joint
teams consisting of both U.S. and Colombian personnel so that the
Colombians get full exposure to on-the-job training; and (d) a price
formula which is satisfactory to the Colombians.

Under the new coal exploration agreement eight Colombians (including two geologists and two engineers) are now working on the
operations. Colombians are also being trained in the United States. A
group of them are now working on a feasibility study for a new mine in
Arkansas as part of the on-the-job training program. One Colombian has
been sent to Canada for two years to head up marketing operations.
The final details of the coal contract are still being worked out. Exxon
is also interested in copper and uranium exploration, and certain dimensions of this wider range of interests may be built into the Colombian
contract.

Peabody Coal, which had had concessionary rights in Colombia for
several years, was offered the same deal as Exxon, but they turned it
down. There were several fundamental differences between the two
companies in corporate outlook and mode of operation. Exxon evolved
into a broad-spectrum mineral and energy corporation, ranging from
exploration and exploitation to international marketing of intermediate
and end-products. Peabody, on the other hand, is exclusively a coal
company with limited international experience. Exxon views coal resources in terms of its energy equivalent, which is now priced at about
one-fourth that of oil. The price and profit-sharing formula worked out
with the Colombians is based upon this perception. In contrast, Peabody values Colombian coal in terms of present mine development cost
and the current market value.

The price formula worked out between Intercol Resources (Exxon's
operating subsidiary for this project) and CARBOCOL (jointly owned
by IFI and ECOPETROL) provides for a forty percent share of returns
to Exxon on basic tonnage mined annually until Exxon recovers its
exploration and mine development costs. Beyond that point Exxon's
share of earnings declines rapidly to five percent. Under the current
arrangements, the foreign partner covers all exploration costs, if no
resource is discovered and exploited. In the event of successful exploitation, the Colombians share in these costs. The Colombian contract was
the first of this type for Exxon. It represents a considerable evolution
in the corporate viewpoint based upon Middle East and Venezuelan
experiences.

U.S. firms still have a pre-eminent position in Colombia. Other foreign groups from Roumania, Brazil, and France are interested but they are generally unwilling to undertake the risks and commitments that U.S. firms such as Exxon are willing to incur. Under the new shareholding arrangements in a joint company, the involved parties are compelled to work together—unlike the protagonist situation typical under the old concessionary arrangements. From Exxon's viewpoint, their retracted financial interest position (now down to $60 million) has reduced political vulnerability. (Additional investments in infrastructure to transport coal will be necessary—about forty percent of $200 million.)

Although Exxon has been in the coal business in the U.S. for fifteen years or more, the Colombian operation represents a new dimension of risk. Unlike Venezuelan oil operations, which are oriented to international markets, the exploitation of the coal resource will depend upon sales to the domestic market, at least initially. There are also considerable problems in transporting the coal from its extraction site in the northeast to the areas where it will be used.

Hanna Mining (Nickel)

Hanna Mining (HM) has had economic interests in Colombia for the past eight years. During this period of time, HM has been involved in the exploration, engineering and start-up of ferro-nickel mining operations. The original deposits were located by Chevron Oil Co., but were turned over to Hanna for further exploration and development. Chevron received a small percent of equity in the final venture.

Throughout this eight-year period, HM and the Colombian Government have been working to achieve a mutually acceptable relationship in the exploration of Colombian nickel resources. Recognizing the changing needs of LDCs, the two parties have negotiated a joint venture which is considered by many international observers to be in the forefront among workable MNC/LDC relationships. The agreement contains the following conditions:

1. Both HM and the Colombian Government hold one-third equity in the joint venture. Chevron Oil owns five percent, and the remainder is divided among a consortium of Japanese and European companies which are nickel consumers, and which will have major production contracts from this concession.

2. HM chose to use World Bank funding for this project. Although private capital resources could have exclusively funded this low-

risk project, HM felt that IBRD intervention would provide an extra degree of financial insurance by an agency which is sensitive to LDC needs and which could exert its influence if needed.

3. The agreement has a life of twenty-five years, although proven reserves under present proposed production output levels are for fifty to seventy-five years. Unless the contract is renegotiated, Colombia will have complete control over a viable mining operation at the end of the agreement.

4. The project provides for basic infrastructural development as well as elective systems of development, so that refining of the ore will take place locally.

5. Technical assistance and technology transfer in a utilizable form is assured. For example, a pilot plant of new design was built in Oregon prior to construction of a full-scale system in Colombia. Thirty Colombian nationals are being trained for periods of up to two years in all aspects of this plant's operation and engineering. A group of U.S. nationals will initially assist the Colombians in operating the full-scale project but the Americans will be phased out in the near term.

6. Project feasibility studies have been undertaken by Bechtel (completed in March 1976), a U.S. corporation; most of the basic engineering work has been delegated to Colombian nationals and a local engineering-consulting firm. The engineering and construction of an electronic furnace involving proprietary technology has been delegated to Elkem Company of Finland.

7. HM has operated in an open manner, sharing its findings, developmental problems, and decision-making with a Colombian committee of eight. Each member has technical expertise in engineering and has had firsthand experience in developing a project to the point of its becoming operational. The committee staff is highly motivated and loyal. They are paid on an internationally competitive basis so that they will not be lured into other countries such as Venezuela. This indicates that the host country recognizes the importance of a favorable environment for its own nationals.[3]

FOOTNOTES

[1]The Andean Code contains three key decisions concerning technological development—Decision 24, 84 and 85. *Decision 24* places restrictions on foreign private investment throughout the Andean region. This decision stipulates that any potential foreign investor must submit an application to a government agency which will determine whether the proposed investment meets the developmental needs of the country. *Decision 84* creates a Subregional Technical Development Policy which mandates that Member Countries establish a scientific and technological infrastructure, establishing linkages between the S & T community and the production units that use technical know-how, through the execution of specific projects, manpower training and information dissemination. *Decision 85* spells out requirements for patents and trademarks.

[2]A similar line of credit was negotiated with the Bank of Mexico. See Chapter III, p. 95 ff. The Colombian fund provided middle term loans for three to seven years at one-third below the commercial rate for the following categories of activities: (a) research and development by the firm or under sub-contract to technical research institutes for new or improved product designs, materials processing, or production techniques; (b) training technicians abroad; (c) payment of visits to Colombia by foreign technicians; (d) purchase of laboratory equipment for quality control and materials testing; (e) lump sum payment for licensing agreements.

[3]In comparison, Peru has similarly recognized the need for highly skilled technical people, but they have not been able to attract and keep them because of pay restrictions and decision-making limitations. Peru's poor record in major projects is in part attributable to the inflexibility of their system.

LIST OF ABBREVIATIONS

CARBOCOL	Colombia Coal Corporation
COLCIENCIAS	Colombian National Fund for Scientific Research and Special Projects
ECONIQUEL	Colombian Nickel Enterprise
ECOPETROL	Colombian Petroleum Enterprise
FICITEC	Foundation for the Promotion of Scientific and Technological Research
IFI	Institute for Industrial Promotion
IIT	Institute for Technological Investigations
INCOMEX	International Trade Institute
SENA	National Training Institute

CHAPTER V
PRACTICAL GUIDELINES FOR THE 1980'S

The previous three chapters reveal a number of significant trends in North-South relations. Prominent among these are national efforts to mobilize resources and develop institutions and mechanisms in support of technological development. Another fundamental theme which emerges is the ever-mounting challenge to traditional modes of foreign business involvement.

The first section in this chapter summarizes the situation in each of the countries and indicates specific policies and measures that would seem appropriate. These individual observations serve to demonstrate that there are important differences among Third World countries, and U.S. policies should be tailored accordingly. At the same time, many of the issues raised are common to other Third World countries, particularly as they relate to their determination to make more effective use of the technology factor for national economic development and to restructure enterprise relationships with industrialized nations to reinforce these new national objectives. The country chapters also provide useful guidelines on measures Third World countries may wish to consider to reinforce the technology factor in national economic development.

The final section sets forth some proposals on new institutional mechanisms designed to facilitate North-South technology transfers within the framework of the realities of the 1980s.

COUNTRY SUMMARIES

Mexico

Recent Mexican experience gives evidence of a new pragmatism in managing institutional arrangements for technological development and in matters concerning international technology transfers. Domestically, there has been a more reasonable balance between efforts to screen and control foreign investment and licensing contracts and efforts to attract foreign enterprise on terms more favorable to the indigenous development of research, design, and engineering capabilities. Mexican authorities also realize that there has been an overemphasis in the past upon developing supply structures for technological support (research institutes and information systems), and that inadequate attention has been paid to reinforcing the demand for technological support from industrial enterprises in the productive sectors. There also has been a relaxing of administrative controls over domestic industry in favor of fiscal measures to increase enterprise incentives to improve operational efficiencies through technical change and adaptation.

Other developments in the Mexican economy relating to trade, investment, and labor market adjustments, point to an expanding need to harmonize commercial and technical relations with the United States. The Mexican economy continues to depend upon the United States in its trade relations—U.S. share is around sixty percent of Mexican exports and imports. At the same time, however, there is a continuing effort to reduce U.S. business influence and control and, wherever possible, to diversify commercial and technical relations. The most recent efforts have been in the direction of seeking to negotiate access to petroleum and natural gas resources in return for industrial technology.

Mexicanization policies (majority ownership of industrial enterprises by Mexican nationals) have been implemented for some time, but substantive managerial control by Mexicans is increasingly evident. Unemployment pressures in Mexico have intensified (up to 300,000 unabsorbed entries into the labor force annually according to one estimate), and the rate of illegal migration into the United States seems to reflect this labor market surplus.

Insofar as new institutional arrangements are concerned, it is true that there is a widespread interest among Mexican entrepreneurs in expanding firm-to-firm contacts with U.S. enterprise as consultative and training sources of design and engineering of products and production systems. There is a general skepticism, however, bordering on suspicion, over the proliferation of proposals put forth unilaterally by the United States.[1] The Mexicans would prefer to consider a more limited number of coordinating and consultative mechanisms that would respond to their expressed interests and needs. Since a major thrust of Mexican policy is enhancement of the bargaining position of Mexican enterprise, part of their suspicion stems from the viewpoint that it is not in the U.S. interest to assist them in this direction. There is marked preference for joint research efforts where Mexican technologies and engineers can participate and benefit from training opportunities.

Bilateral Agreements. Under the previous administration, the movement was away from bilateral agreements with the U.S. toward multinational arrangements through diversified channels in Canada, Western Europe and Japan. Under the new administration, Mexican officials seem to be especially interested in extending previous bilateral agreements to areas that reinforce applied research efforts in support of industrial enterprise activities. They also would like to move beyond university level interchange to joint research and scientific programs directly linked to enterprise problems and needs. PEMEX (Mexican Petroleum Corporation) is especially interested in joint programs in scientific fields related to petrochemical technology and direct links with U.S. corporations. They now have certain arrangements with firms such as Universal Oil Products (UOP). CONACYT is anxious to expand its role as an intermediary with university-based research and scientific training. Several officials indicated they also would like to see a shifting emphasis on developing scientific and technical manpower that would contribute to the development of indigenous design and engineering capabilities in local R&D projects.

Firm-to-Firm Cooperation. Certain government officials and enterprise representatives favored institutional mechanisms that would facilitate an expansion of firm-to-firm contacts between Mexico and the U.S. They are interested in U.S. firms that can provide process technology, new or improved product designs, technical assistance on machinery purchase and utilization, technical information (particularly of a nondocumented nature), and other technical support services. It is not clear what the marketing arrangements for such services would be. One possibility is that these technical services could be tied to purchase contracts (as in cases of automotive components purchased by Mexican subsidiaries of U.S. vehicle manufacturers for export to the U.S.). Mexican firms are interested in both practical consulting on design and operational problems and in having extended access to industrial technology in the U.S.

The foregoing trends and considerations would seem to indicate that the U.S. should respond to this new pragmatism with flexibility and do so in a spirit of enlightened self-interest. This would imply acceptance of minority positions in Mexican enterprise, yielding of managerial control to Mexican nationals, and expanded willingness to share technology and market opportunities with Mexican enterprises. In considering new institutional mechanisms, the emphasis should be on facilitating firm-to-firm contacts between U.S. and Mexican enterprises—for example, in assisting them to develop export capabilities which absorb Mexican labor without threatening U.S. industrial jobs. Some Mexican firms are in a position to expand into industrial sectors that are in irreversible decline in the U.S.—certain foundry work, for example.

The United States should explore the advantage and feasibility of bilateral trade negotiations that take into account Mexico's need to expand its export earnings in the manufacturing sector and the desire on the part of Mexican firms to enlarge and enhance their competitiveness in world markets. U.S. programs in support of Mexican industry can contribute to difficult labor market adjustment problems on both sides of the border. These bilateral consultations might include targeted offset trading (expansion of exports of manufactured goods from Mexico) to cover Mexico's trade deficits and to help generate jobs in Mexico so as to reduce illegal labor migration pressures. (See below, U.S.-Mexican Common Market.) Proposed institutional mechanisms which identify U.S. firms willing to share technology and markets with Mexican firms on a mutually advantageous basis would be especially useful in alleviating the above problems.

In the area of "appropriate technology," the U.S. should refrain from foisting its views on Mexico. Certain U.S. officials take the view that the extensive application of labor-intensive technologies will provide the answer to the illegal migration of Mexican labor—a viewpoint to which Mexican officials take strong exception. There are undoubtedly some opportunities for additional labor absorption through "appropriate technology" but at least equal attention should be directed to the Mexican viewpoint of export expansion as a job-generating channel.

U.S.-Mexican Common Market. Mexican government officials expressed an interest in bilateral consultative mechanisms that would link technology search and contract negotiation with U.S. firms with trade and industrial employment (and illegal labor migration) problems. On the other hand in response to its interest, the United States should consider negotiating a special trade agreement somewhat along the lines of the U.S.-Canadian Automotive Agreement, under which certain targeted levels of two-way imports and exports (stated in value-added terms) in designated product areas are negotiated in advance between the two countries on an annual basis. Under the proposed arrangements, the U.S. would offset U.S.-Mexican trade deficits through the expansion of imports of manufactured goods from Mexico in designated industries that do not pose a threat to U.S. production employment. This export expansion would offer opportunities for industrial employment expansion in the Mexican economy, particularly in small-to-medium enterprise where the labor expansion factor per unit of value added is often the highest.

A joint U.S.-Mexican Commission could be established to designate industrial product groups in which trade is to be expanded, to set targeted levels of trade expansion, and to establish the role for U.S.-Mexican enterprise involvement in the new trading arrangements.

In the latter area, ongoing arrangements already exist in the Mexican automotive industry, where U.S. vehicle manufacturers in Mexico are required to meet certain automotive parts export quotas in order to maintain their shares in Mexico. Reference was made in Chapter III to existing arrangements between U.S. and Mexican firms under which the former uses the latter as a procurement source for certain export demand to help pay for U.S. sales of goods and services (including production technology). (See reference to Gray Tool Company/Epsna, III.)

Brazil

Brazilian authorities have been fairly explicit concerning their technological development goals and the institutional means to carry out stated objectives. In their bilateral arrangements with the United States, they seek to strengthen Brazilian capacity in the fields of research and development. They want to augment the flow of U.S. technology for the solution of specific industrial problems or for initial entry into new industrial areas, (such as new processing technology for their energy and mineral resources).

From an institutional point of view, they would like to use both U.S. public institutions as well as private enterprise capabilities to improve Brazilian productive capacity and supporting technological infrastructure. They also would like to increase domestic activities in the field of research and development; to further intensify the use of indigenous technologies; to adapt the imported technology to innovation requirements, economic conditions and Brazilian productive capacity; and to build up the necessary scientific and technological agencies for research, standards, quality control, metrology and technology evaluation. It is clear that Brazil intends to multilateralize its commercial, technical, and trade relations with Europe, Japan, socialist countries, and other newly industrializing nations, with a view toward enhancing their bargaining power for technology by reducing their overdependence on U.S. technology sources.

Balance-of-payment difficulties and the related foreign exchange constraint impinge upon the Brazilian counterpart funding of bilateral arrangements with the U.S. in the science and technology field. Any effort on the U.S. part to alleviate this difficulty would be regarded by the Brazilians as a real token of constructive friendship. The Brazilian Government would much prefer to fund science and technology programs on a sector basis, rather than along project lines, through international lending agencies such as the World Bank and the Inter-American Development Bank. In fact, they would prefer to negotiate broad trade, industrial development, and technical assistance agreements along the lines concluded with the German Government in the nuclear technology field.

It would be well to remember that Brazil has long encountered negative responses to its aspirations for technological development from the United States. For example, in the late forties, Brazil was flatly denied access to U.S. steel technology for its Volta Redonda complex, and it was forced to turn to Krupp of Germany. Twenty-five years later, a similar scenario took place surrounding Brazil's desire to acquire the know-how to produce nuclear energy. It is true that the latter contained broader and graver implications for the United States, but both instances dramatically illustrate, in the Brazilian view, an arrogance and myopia on the part of the United States. It is perhaps worthwhile to remember that technology acquisition and technological development are viewed as vital to the national interest, and a continued tendency on the part of the United States to underestimate or overlook this fact would be counter-productive.

The energy development problem is representative of the type of deep dilemmas involving the mobilization of technology resources with which Brazil is now confronted. In order to meet its enormously expanded energy needs over the next decades without adding to its already over-burdened balance-of-payments position, Brazil must either develop new technology to transmit electricity economically over vast distances or develop the technological base for deriving energy from nuclear or other non-conventional sources. In the past, the United States understandably has expressed concern over the military and strategic implications of nuclear proliferation, but it cannot disregard the legitimate and equally understandable efforts on the Brazilian side to help resolve certain long-term economic difficulties through the progressive build-up of national technological capabilities which requires ready sources of energy.

Whether or not the Brazilians are over-ambitious in their technological development programs—attempting to do too much in too short a time—is in part a matter of judgment. A number of Brazilians, in fact, have expressed certain doubts and reservations in this regard. Such judgments, however, would wisely be removed from U.S. policy toward Brazil on purely pragmatic grounds, given the country's demonstrated determination to carry out the programs, with or without U.S. approval or support.

In view of the foregoing, the United States should seek to strike a balance between a sympathetic understanding of Brazilian aspirations and what is reasonably and realistically achievable on a mutually advantageous basis. Above all, the United States should demonstrate flexibility in considering new requests—particularly in the area of Brazilian enterprise development—recognizing that new business arrangements are being negotiated with U.S. enterprise that meet emerging Brazilian needs and are at the same time responsive to commercial realities.

The evolving patterns of industrialization in Brazil call for some adjustment in U.S. business and government attitudes toward the role of U.S. private investment and modes of U.S. business enterprise involvement abroad. The position that an owned and controlled subsidiary is the only viable means of industrial technology transfer is no longer tenable. This viewpoint needs to be modified to accommodate the new realities of national development objectives and newly negotiated arrangements between U.S. firms and Brazilian enterprise groups. In matters involving negotiations for technology transfers between U.S. and Brazilian enterprises, the United States Government should refrain from interceding on behalf of U.S. firms that are attempting to maintain a strong front against technology release (as mentioned in the aircraft and computer cases). These negotiations should be left to the marketplace and to the legal framework established in Brazil; any effort on the U.S. part to intercede will only exacerbate commercial and political relations between the two countries, and Brazil will increasingly look for trading partners elsewhere in the world.

On the subject of realistic accommodations that the U.S. can make in response to Brazil's expressed technological development needs, there are several possibilities. In the area of bilateral agreements for interchange of research personnel and technical information, the Brazilians are especially interested in firm-to-firm cooperation on a reimbursable technical assistance basis. They are especially interested in soft-loan financing of the foreign exchange component of such programs. The Brazilians have pointed out in their encounters with U.S. officials that although both governments "have found reciprocal cooperation profitable," interchange programs have actually declined due to the decrease of resources on the American side, including the phasing out of U.S. AID funding of programs by the U.S. National Academy of Sciences.

One Brazilian complaint has been that the U.S. has been unwilling to fund foreign exchange costs for Brazilians participating in research projects in the U.S. and for training fellowships. The Brazilians also have sought to negotiate more favorable financial terms on purchased research equipment. A final point raised by the Brazilians concerned the lack of coordination mechanisms on the U.S. side involving American institutions other than the National Science Foundation and other U.S. Government agencies. The Brazilians indicated their interest in reinforcing linkages to U.S. sources of scientific and technological information and improving financial arrangements for the purchase of research laboratory equipment. They also reaffirmed their interest and desire in expanding training of research personnel in designated fields.

Brazilians are especially interested in study and research experience in the U.S. At the Amazon Research Center in Manaus, the effects of bilateral agreements were evident in the number of American scientists working on various tropical ecology problems, including tropical diseases and environmental management of the Amazon River. There is an active U.S.-Brazilian bilateral agreement in the area of space research with the Institute for Space Research (INPE) and with the Brazilian Commission for Space Activities (COBAE), with overall coordination under the National Council on Scientific and Technological Development (CNPq). In the aeronautics and space exploration field, there are close linkages of the research and educational communities with the production sector (this includes both aircraft production and the manufacture of space probe rockets). The existence of these linkages is important to ensure a rapid and effective benefit from the training of scientists and engineers.

Insofar as programs to reach poorer segments of the Brazilian population are concerned—a subject on which the Brazilians have been highly sensitive when it comes to U.S. foreign assistance—a constructive approach might be to explore applications involving U.S. technology and know-how in the area of nutrition, health, and human welfare. For example, one small U.S. firm was involved in a program to manufacture and distribute low-cost optical goods in Brazil. (See reference below to Small Enterprise Development Corporation.)

In the field of energy, the U.S. Government has an interest in joint programs that could benefit both economies—particularly in the area of low-emission automotive engine designs that are fuel-efficient. The U.S. Department of Transportation has a particular interest in this area (it has a contract with Volkswagen in Germany for engine development along these lines), and consultation with Brazilian counterparts in this area may be in order.

Colombia

The insights and recommendations that follow derive from the particular set of conditions encountered in Colombia and the special set of possibilities they represent for U.S. response. Colombia's developmental goals place a special emphasis upon raising the living standards of the rural and urban poor, and mechanisms to assist the Colombian Government in this area would be especially appropriate, in view of our own Government's interest in reorienting foreign aid to benefit low-income groups. (See reference below to Enterprise Frontiers to Benefit the Rural and Urban Poor.)

A second area of priority concern to the Colombian Government is the expansion of domestic manufacture for export, especially by small-to-medium industry, where the employment effects may be maximized. In order to advance this sector, the Colombians are in particular need of technical inputs to upgrade the productivity and competitiveness of small-to-medium industry. As in the case of Mexico, they need the linkages to American firms to provide some of the technical upgrading of product designs, production techniques and managerial personnel, as well as entries into U.S. and other export markets. Mechanisms and institutional arrangements that would provide these business linkages and export entries would be especially appropriate.

The mineral and energy sector is a third area of prime concern to the development authorities in Colombia. Mechanisms and institutional arrangements that expand their technological absorptive capabilities and ability to move toward progressive self-reliance in managing the exploitation of their natural resources would be particularly welcomed.

There is an identified need for institutional arrangements that will improve the technological absorptive capabilities of Colombian enterprise and their access to foreign technology components, including the training of industrial managers and technologists. The Colombians are particularly receptive to proposals to enhance access to foreign technical information and to provide direct foreign technical support to Colombian enterprises.

In view of the foregoing, it would be advisable for the United States to continue to pursue policies that are sensitive and sympathetic to national aspirations for progressive technological self-sufficiency in the mineral and energy field. It should take cognizance of the fact that whereas certain firms have had difficulty in accommodating to the changing environment in Colombia, others have found ways to do business on a mutually acceptable and advantageous basis. Efforts to extend business contacts with U.S. firms to assist Colombian enterprise toward technological self-sufficiency should not be discouraged or inhibited, but viewed rather as part of the legitimate effort of a newly industrializing nation to improve its economic position and political bargaining power in a changing world economy.

One possibility in this regard would be the establishment by the U.S. Government of a Small Enterprise Development Corporation (see below). The proposed SEDC would address itself to promoting employment-generating projects for the rural and urban poor and should be given special attention for its application to the Colombian situation. As indicated in the recommendations for Mexico, the United States should stand prepared to assist in this area, rather than to attempt to foist its concepts and approaches. We also should explore with the Colombian Government its interest in new modes of firm-to-firm cooperation to assist Colombian-managed enterprise in its efforts to upgrade technologically and to further expand into world markets on a mutually advantageous basis. The proposal for a Technology Transfer Service Corporation (see below) might be further explored in this regard.

GUIDELINES TO THIRD WORLD POLICIES AND INITIATIVES

The various measures a government may wish to consider may be broken down into functional groups: to plan the technology component of product systems; to carry out research, design and engineering functions; to search and negotiate for technology from foreign sources; to carry out technical supporting services and training; and to utilize acquired technology in terms of installation, operation, and maintenance of systems.

The previous chapters describe a variety of institutional means to: (a) restructure the supply of technology (largely through the screening and control of technology acquisitions from foreign sources); (b) restructure the internal demand for technology (through reinforcement of planning, searching and negotiating capabilities at the public institution and enterprise levels); and (c) reinforce the absorptive infrastructure (through training of key personnel in the use and generation of technology and related support systems).

The particular combination of measures a country may choose to undertake will depend upon a broad variety of factors, including: the stage of industrial development; the level of industrial entrepreneurship; the degree to which market mechanisms encourage and promote private sector initiative; and the effectiveness of existing institutional mechanisms involved in financial, research, and other support capabilities at the enterprise level, which constitute the critical link in technological development.

Both Brazil and Mexico have begun to move away from strong

emphasis on screening and control of the supply of technology from foreign sources toward more effective ways to reinforce the demand for technology (in terms of the ability to search for and select technology among alternative sources and to negotiate on favorable terms for technology) and to reinforce technological absorptive capabilities at the national enterprise level. National technological development objectives are increasingly focusing on the restructuring of effective demand for the technology component of productive systems to create or reinforce supporting infrastructure, such as design and engineering firms, technical research institutes and laboratories, and capital goods industries that can design and manufacture machines and equipment more suitable to the country's emerging needs and conditions.

Technological capabilities to reinforce the absorptive infrastructure vary widely among countries and are far more difficult to manage than the creation of screening and control mechanisms. Development authorities in the three countries surveyed now perceive that the major obstacles to technological self-sufficiency lie not so much in knowing what they do not want and keeping it out, but in knowing what they do want and need, and how to acquire it on favorable terms and to use it effectively. National legislation and budgeted expenditures have not proven to be the most effective means for achieving desired results.

Brazil has been the most successful in planning, searching and negotiating for the technology component of its national development. This includes efforts to assure that foreign technology acquired from abroad is first, needed, and second, obtained on favorable terms. Mexico has also been comparatively successful in this area, but due mostly to large private Mexican conglomerates which have well developed capabilities in performing the aforementioned functions. In Colombia, the new associated agreements also represent a significant advance in this area.

The principal infrastructural deficiencies in all three countries relate either to shortages in trained technical personnel and/or to inadequate linkages between research communities and productive enterprises. Colombia is relatively well endowed in technical and entrepreneurial capabilities at the enterprise level. While Mexico has a relatively well developed supporting and absorptive infrastructure, immense unemployment problems pose a unique set of pressures on the economy to upgrade technological absorptive capabilities so as to accelerate growth, create jobs, and generate income. Brazil appears to be progressing rapidly in its efforts to establish a strong technological base from which foreign technology is absorbed and adapted, new technologies are generated, and training and support services are made available at the enterprise level.

The major means for implementing technology programs have been: (a) the use of state enterprises in basic industries—with Brazil in the forefront of efforts, followed closely by Mexico and Colombia; (b) government funding of science and technology programs—in which area Brazil has made major efforts; (c) financial mechanisms in support of technology objectives—in which area Brazil probably stands in the forefront, followed by Mexico; and (d) government controls over international transfer of technology—an area where all three governments have been active. (Figure V-1 provides an overview of Inter-Country Comparisons of Institutional Means to Manage Technological Development.)

Negotiation for Technology Acquisitions

The ability of Third World enterprises to negotiate advantageous technology-sharing agreements in identified opportunity areas will depend upon: (a) the bargaining leverage and enterprise strategies of the technology supplier; (b) the bargaining leverage and enterprise strategies of the technology purchaser; (c) the supporting programs and policies of the purchaser government; and (d) the distinctive characteristics of the transferred technology. (See Figure V-2.)

Possible commercial, technical and financial strategies motivating the supplier enterprise to share technology, along with the various elements which contribute to its bargaining position, are listed in the first column of the model. Similarly, purchaser strategies and sources of bargaining leverage are listed in the third column of the model.

The ultimate viability and success of any technology transfer and implantation are heavily dependent upon the level of support extended by the government to the purchaser enterprise. There has been an increasing determination on the part of Third World governments to intervene in the negotiation process to assure favorable contractual terms for national enterprise and to provide further reinforcement in the implantation stage. Included here are: (a) the protection of infant or national industry against foreign imports; (b) technical support networks and institutions to assist the purchasing enterprise in the production and marketing function; and (c) making available necessary credit and foreign exchange needed to purchase equipment and expert training.

The potential value of a technology package[2] to a purchaser and the adjustment problems it poses are a function of the distinctive characteristics of the technology supplied. We have listed some of these major characteristics of technology in the middle column of the model and describe them more fully in the remaining portion of this section. Ele-

FIGURE V-1. INTER-COUNTRY COMPARISONS OF INSTITUTIONAL
MEANS TO MANAGE TECHNOLOGICAL DEVELOPMENT

FUNCTION	COUNTRY		
	BRAZIL	MEXICO	COLOMBIA
Restructuring Supply of Technology (Screening and Control)	Federal regulation of technology agreements. State ownership of enterprise in priority sectors.	Registry of Foreign Investment. Registry of Technology Transfer. Regulations on patents and trademarks.	Decisions 24 and 85 of Cartagena Agreement (ANCOM) regulations. Private Investment Division of National Planning Department.
Restructuring Internal Demand for Technology (Planning, Searching, and Negotiating)	Heavy state involvement assures complementarity between demand and national objectives. Well developed search and negotiation capabilities at public and large private enterprise levels.	Large national enterprise and Mexican-controlled joint ventures proficient in obtaining technology on favorable terms. Weak capability among small and medium enterprise. Limited government assistance in cited capabilities.	Evolving capability in energy and mineral resource management.
Reinforcing Absorptive Infrastructure for Technology (Training, Supporting, Using, and Generating)	Strong network of supporting institutions associated with state-run enterprises. Using and generating capabilities are comparatively strong. Contracts with foreign firms designed to enhance cited capabilities.	Strong capability among large national conglomerates. Weak linkages between science-technology enterprise communities.	Associated agreements designs to upgrade absorptive capability. Evolving capabilities among small-to-medium enterprises.

FIGURE V-2. ANALYTICAL FRAMEWORK: TECHNOLOGY SHARING BY U.S.-BASED MULTINATIONALS WITH DEVELOPING WORLD NATIONS

TECHNOLOGY SUPPLIER	TECHNOLOGY PACKAGE	TECHNOLOGY PURCHASER
• Bargaining Leverage Competitive world market position. Technological lead. Negotiating astuteness. Financial resources.	• Distinctive Characteristics Quantum and complexity. License to manufacture or turnkey-plus. Operative, duplicative, or innovative. General-, firm-, or system-specific stage in product/process cycle.	• Bargaining Leverage Reinforcing government support. National resource endowment. Financial and foreign exchange. Attractive national market. Technological absorptive capabilities. Alternative sources of technology.
• Enterprise Strategies Returns from technology sales provide funds to maintain technology lead. Continued access to lucrative market. Possibility of future low-cost procurement source. Continued access to scarce resources.	• Supporting Government Policies Screening and control mechanisms. Technical support networks. Acting as the negotiation and purchasing agent. Infant industry protection.	• Enterprise Strategies Obtain internationally competitive technology. Entry into export markets. Fast, efficient technology transfer plants. Duplicative and/or innovative design and engineering capabilities. Training of technical-managerial manpower.

ments of the technology package, which include technical data and human skills, are conveyed through an interactive process of adjusting implanted procedures and equipment operation until the desired production efficiencies and quality standards are achieved.

The effectiveness of technology transfers depends in large part upon the absorptive capabilities of the recipient enterprise and the industrial environment in which it operates, and to a lesser extent upon the transfer capabilities of the technology supplier. A basic reason for acquiring technology from another enterprise (rather than through one's own research and development) is that it is generally much cheaper and quicker[3] —which is the reason why technology has become a "commodity" in world trade.

Another critical aspect relevant to international technology transfers is the distinction between implanting "operational" (turnkey) technology and imparting technical capabilities to duplicate that technology, which, in some cases, may lead to an indigenous capability to design and engineer industrial systems. The Japanese have been particularly successful in using licensing arrangements as stepping stones to self-sufficient technological capabilities, which were eventually used to develop new generations of internationally competitive products, processes, and production systems. Achieving worthwhile results in the latter area depends, in part, on the state of development of the recipient enterprise and supporting industrial sectors.

NEW INSTITUTIONAL MECHANISMS TO FACILITATE NORTH-SOUTH TECHNOLOGY TRANSFERS[4]

Technology Transfer Service Corporation (TTSC)

A major deficiency in U.S.-Latin American technology transfers is the lack of appropriate financial mechanisms to bridge the gap between would-be (U.S.) supplier firms unable or unwilling to become venture capitalists and Latin American enterprises seeking technology packages which will meet the new sets of national goals for technological development and which will increase capabilities to diagnose technological adjustment problems and to participate in the adjustment and absorption process at the enterprise level.

Most of the technology acquired by Latin American enterprises from U.S. sources has been under investment and licensing arrangements with U.S. firms in the Fortune 1000 group—and most of these are subsidiaries or joint venture companies. As we have seen, the demands for technology have far exceeded supplier response for a number of fundamental reasons relating to the expanded role of the technology factor in development as explained in each of the country chapters.

One of the reasons why the supply of technology from American enterprise sources has been restricted is the fact that only a limited number of U.S. firms are in a position financially, and from a risk-taking standpoint, even to explore business opportunities in Latin America, let alone to pay for technology transfer costs well in advance of realized earnings. (It may be several years before an overseas business venture in a developing world country breaks even and begins to yield a return.) Even under licensing arrangements without equity involvement, there are the risks, uncertainties and time delays associated with royalty payments. Few licensor firms are in a position to incur the additional costs of technical support services that may be associated with the successful implant of operationally efficient industrial technology. These additional costs involve adjustments in product designs, production engineering, and in manufacturing practices, which are typically required for particular market conditions and operational environments.

Another factor inhibiting technology sales is the reluctance of most banks to finance the "intangibles" of technology acquisition (design, engineering, training, and related manufacturing implant services) on both the purchaser and supplier sides. Neither private commercial banks nor government-sponsored development banks are willing, or in some instances able, to lend for local enterprise expenditures on technological upgrading. A new set of financial mechanisms are needed which can accommodate the categories of expenditures for "intangibles," apart from the sale of capital equipment and for similar five-year terms.[5]

U.S. commercial banks and the Export-Import Bank, by and large, do not provide the short-term and medium-term supplier credit needed for the type of technology transfer contracts generally sought by Third World enterprises. Shortcomings and deficiencies in this regard are delineated in what follows and serve as the basis and background for recommendations that appear in the succeeding section.

1. A fundamental problem is that most U.S. commercial banks are much more conservative than European or Japanese banks in extending credit for foreign trade in general, and their conservatism extends back to the U.S. Government-sponsored mechanisms intended to promote export trade by the Export-Import Bank and the associated Foreign Credit Insurance Agency (FCIA).

2. The above-mentioned financial conservatism is especially pronounced when it comes to lending for service intangibles, except where sales are associated with the export of equipment and/or connected with large scale construction projects. The reluctance to lend for these purposes is traceable in part to difficulties in the defining and pricing of services and in certifying delivery and adequate performance under such contracts.

3. Technology transfer arrangements exist between Third World enterprises and U.S. firms with annual sales in the $5-to-50-million range. The latter may be experienced manufacturers in the U.S., but are only now beginning to enter export markets as technology transfer agents. In the eyes of lending institutions and payment guarantee insurers (Eximbank and FCIA), this heightens the risk factor in terms of the creditworthiness of the purchaser and the performance capability of the U.S. firm supplying technology services.

4. The size of loans associated with technology transfers are small relative to machine and equipment purchases, and the vetting of these contracts are more complicated. Both of these factors contribute to increased unit overhead costs for loan processing, and therefore commercial banks tend to shy away from them.

The central objective of the proposed TTSC would be to expand involvement of U.S. firms with under U.S.$100 million sales annually.[6] The TTSC is designed to accommodate the widespread demands in Latin America (and other developing world nations) for manufacturing know-how and related design engineering and other technical support services without the management and control normally involved in the foreign investment by large multinational firms. The TTSC would provide growth opportunities to a broad spectrum of U.S. firms. Many of these firms are in need of financial resources to upgrade and expand existing production lines which are no longer internationally competitive, and they can use these additional earnings to reinforce and expand their current design-engineering capabilities and to upgrade existing plant and equipment.

The proposed TTSC is conceived as a small, autonomous group to promote, finance, and help implement technology service exports. The TTSC would operate initially in selected newly industrializing countries, under cooperative agreements negotiated with appropriate development banking intermediaries. These cooperative groups would: (a) determine technology survey requirements; (b) develop project profiles of technology requirements; and (c) determine creditworthiness of local enterprise groups. Among other functions, TTSC would: (a) translate these requirements into cost estimates for required services; (b) identify and select suitable U.S. enterprise candidates to supply the required technology transfer services; (c) make arrangements for field visits by U.S. firms to complete contract arrangements; and (d) arrange for financing of project.

Small Enterprise Development Corporation (SEDC)

Urban and rural poor populations face particularly difficult, and often intractable circumstances when it comes to improving their economic conditions. Too often, overall industrial expansion does little to benefit them through increases in jobs, income, and needed goods. The establishment of new enterprise forms, including self-managed enterprises, may be one way to give the poor new access to decision-making and control of the means of production, and consequent income-earning opportunities. In other cases, it may prove possible to link together small-scale enterprise or artisan groups to achieve economies of scale in purchasing, marketing, distribution, storing, bookkeeping, and for other legal/technical/management services. These new enterprise forms could reach large numbers of people with greater effectiveness from a social development viewpoint. These various new enterprise forms could provide additional opportunities to increase productivity among this group of income earners and to increase their share of income from value added in production units.

A Small Enterprise Development Corporation (SEDC), specially staffed to reach into the sub-cultures of poor populations, with an appropriate line of credit, may be one means to improve the earning power and security of the poor. Traditional credit institutions, even those oriented to small-scale enterprise, are ineffective in this area. They are unable to assist in the indispensable task of project formulation that an SEDC would be staffed to undertake and are either unable or unwilling to administer the large number of small loans for numerous small projects that are typical of this sector. Development banks generally are unwilling to take the inevitable risks that characterize this area. Special skills will be required to start these projects and to monitor the experiments, until they reach a point of viability—especially self-managed projects.

The SEDC would operate as an autonomous public corporation

with funding from national and international sources. Its functions would include the following:

1. To develop access and ties to urban poor communities, with a view toward involving them in project formulation and other steps in the decision process.

2. To establish appropriate linkages with public agencies (national and international) that could provide funding, programming, or technical support.

3. To identify and help formulate projects for the poor.

4. To establish liaison with local agencies and groups that can assist in project formulation and execution—including training, technical support, appropriate technology design, marketing, and other necessary ancillary support services.

5. To monitor funded projects with a view toward improving the impact of lending.

6. To help syndicate loans with other lending institutions for projects that have passed the incubation stage.

Other Mechanisms to Assist Technical Development of Small-to-Medium Enterprise

There are several additional areas in which programs to assist small-scale enterprise development could be initiated or expanded. Among the possibilities are: (a) subcontracting and government procurement systems to provide new market linkages and to channel technical support to small enterprises; (b) industrial estates and cooperatives to help small-scale enterprises compete more effectively; (c) special technology funds that link technical assistance with credit sources; and (c) demonstration and technical service centers.

A subcontracting system that extends—or can be persuaded to extend—down to the informal sector is a potentially useful mechanism for expanding small-scale enterprise operations. The subcontracting system can provide new market linkages—both internal and external—as well as serve as a mode of enterprise-to-enterprise technology transfer. As part of industrial subcontracting arrangements, purchasers of materials and parts are often willing to provide a full range of technical support information and manufacturing know-how in order to ensure a quality-controlled end product. In addition to supplying drawings and blue-prints, the contractor firm may provide training in specialized techniques and quality control, or lease special tooling and other equipment to subcontractors.

Government procurement programs are another major production generating means, since the public sector represents a major purchaser of goods and services. Through a local procurement system (in such products or sub-assemblies as school furniture and simple hospital equipment) Third World governments can assist small-scale enterprises by providing an initial demand for their products. These programs should be designed with a view toward overcoming certain deficiencies, primarily in the areas of technical upgrading, marketing, and production organization and management. An ancillary support system, including a liaison at the ministry level to coordinate such efforts, may also be needed to ensure program success.

Another method of expanding and upgrading small-scale enterprise operations is to create industrial estates, where common industrial facilities are shared by several small-to-medium firms. Within such estates, labor-intensive production units may be encouraged through support services including technical advice, common facilities, training of technical personnel, design and development of equipment production techniques and quality control. Industrial estates could be organized in coordination with a government procurement system.

Industrial cooperatives, similar to industrial estates, are another effective means through which small firms are able to upgrade and expand technical capabilities. Technical assistance may come from outside the cooperative or from training centers within it. Cooperatives may offer services such as planning, manpower training, research, bulk purchasing, joint processing facilities, repair shops, and business and technical advice. Industrial cooperatives have been successful in over sixty LDCs.

A technology fund also could be effective in upgrading small-scale rural and urban enterprises. Various technical assistance groups could act as intermediaries between small enterprises and the technology fund—for the identification of projects, assistance in the formulation of proposals, and support in their implementation.

Another useful institutional support mechanism is the "demonstration," or industrial extension center. Small-scale producers located in remote town-centered or urban slums, operating under relatively primitive conditions and with little sophistication in production management, could derive great benefit from such centers. Demonstration centers can provide basic assistance in rationalizing inefficient operations and can help to introduce more efficient production methods, quality control systems and equipment designs. These programs would be aimed at enhancing market opportunities or increasing cost competitiveness of small-scale enterprise. Demonstration centers can identify production deficiencies within a particular industry and develop improvements in product designs, production methods, and materials or equipment utilization, which they can then demonstrate to small enterprises engaged in related industrial activities.

Technical support centers can serve in a variety of ways to assist small-scale enterprises in the areas of technical upgrading, marketing, and production organization and management. Their activities could complement or be part of the demonstration center. Their primary services could include: (a) technical advice on adapting and upgrading technology; (b) instruction on production organization and management of the small enterprise; (c) the provision of common facilities, such as tool and die-making, heat treatment, electric plating, and small tool accessories; (d) training of technical personnel; (e) design and development of equipment, production techniques, and packaging; and (f) formulation of technical standards.

A secondary service that could be provided by the technical support center is to act as an institutional link or intermediary, between the small enterprise and government procurement or subcontracting systems, and between the enterprise and sources of financing. The technical support center is the natural agency for promoting subcontracting or government procurement between large and small industries. Its daily contact with small enterprises would place it in a unique position to gather information not only on the machinery and equipment available in small units, but also on their skills, specializations, and quality of production. The center should be able to publicize information on subcontracting or government procurement opportunity. It should be able to systematically collect and keep up-to-date information and serve as a clearinghouse to bring together supply and demand for such operations. The center could establish contact with large enterprises to find out which parts and components are required, and circulate lists of small firms capable of filling these orders.

CONCLUDING REMARKS

An implicit assumption in our findings is that part of the problem of accommodation is the lag in perceptions of a changing world. There is also a reluctance on both sides to face up to the reality of change and to accept the necessity to reconcile differences if mutually destructive conflict is to be avoided. A basic purpose of this book has been to provide insights and guidelines leading to practical arrangements that will contribute to conflict resolution. Hopefully, these suggestions will lead to realistic accommodations of conflicts between the United States and the Third World country interests. The empirical insights summarized in this last chapter and the accompanying proposals for institutional arrangements should prove very useful in moving toward mutually advantageous courses of action, rather than continuing recriminations and mutually detrimental behavior.

An additional note of caution is worth remark. Policy makers all too often are looking for blueprints that promise instant success. There are no such blueprints. At best, what we can hope for are insightful diagnoses of predicaments, followed by experimental efforts on a trial and error basis. The proposed institutional mechanisms therefore should be regarded as "sketches" rather than "blueprints." As a famous French general once remarked, *"On s'engage, et puis on verra."*

FOOTNOTES

[1]Institutional trial balloons have included the Resource Development Bank, Technology Corps, and a plethora of other proposals.

[2]Technology may be defined as the "package" of product designs, production and processing techniques, and managerial systems that are used to manufacture particular industrial products. A modern diesel truck engine consists of approximately 750 individual parts and requires over 30,000 separate steps to convert industrial materials (over 350 different kinds) into finished components. The technology package consists of detailed process sheets, materials, specifications, processing and testing equipment designations, and quality-control procedures. Together they are a measure of the "quantum and complexity" of a technology transplant. These tens of thousands of elements for a single industrial product, such as a high-speed diesel, are meticulously accumulated over time through research and development, through trial and error in equipment and factory methods, and in the detailed specifications and procedures developed through prolonged experience. The quantum and complexity of technology in certain high technology fields, such as computers and jet aircraft, become ever greater.

[3]The foregoing observation leads to an important distinction that needs to be drawn among "firm-specific," "system-specific," and "general" technology. The first refers to the tried-and-tested practical knowledge that a firm has developed over time to produce a particular product—with all the bits and pieces fitting together and functioning at a cost-competitive level. "System-specific" refers to specialized capabilities that a firm may have developed over time in such areas as welding techniques (for example, to attach the fins of a turbojet engine to the drive shaft) or casting techniques for a special alloy (of high quality without porosity for the same turbojet engine). "General" knowledge is the easily obtained, nondetailed information about design and manufacturing principles for, say, fractional horsepower electrical motors.

[4]Insights and recommendations based upon special report prepared by author of Science and Technology Policy on New Mechanisms to Facilitate the Sale of Technology by U.S. Enterprises to Newly Industrializing Nations (October 1980).

[5]There have been a number of experimental efforts to fill the above described needs for special lines of financial credits. The author has been instrumental in establishing on an experimental basis, technology improvement funds in Mexico, Colombia, and Turkey. These funds are

for on-lending to local enterprises to finance the intangibles of technology acquisition and adjustment.

[6]There are approximately 300,000 manufacturing firms in the U.S., of which approximately 800 U.S. corporations account for over ninety-five percent of investments and licensing agreements.

APPENDIX
SYNOPSIS OF BRAZIL'S ORDINANCE 15

The Industrial National Property Institute (INPI) has established new regulations for the transfer of technology into Brazil, as expressed in Ordinance 15. Technology transfer agreements are put into five categories: (1) patent license agreements; (2) trademark license agreements; (3) industrial technology license agreements; (4) technical and industrial cooperation agreements; and (5) technical service agreements. Each type of agreement must be registered with INPI in accordance with different regulations.

1. Patent license agreements are defined as contracts which are aimed at authorizing the effective use by third parties of patents granted or deposited in Brazil, involving title to industrial property (as defined under the Brazilian Property Code). Such agreements also include the supply of know-how (materials, designs, models, processes and similar data), and technical assistance.

Remuneration for a patent by the licensee to licensor is based on: (a) the degree of essentiality of the patent; (b) the start of the patent's effective use; and (c) the sale of the product derived from the patent. If a patent is transferred, the price may be a fixed amount. Payment for technical documentation provided for in the patent license agreement may be considered as advance payment of the total remuneration. Computation of the remuneration due to individual technicians will be based on the number of technicians, an accepted "per diem" price, and an estimate of the period of time required to render the technical assistance. Each type of patent license agreement has its own legal term of validity under current legislation: invention patents—up to fifteen years; industrial model patents—up to ten years; industrial design patents—up to ten years.

2. Trademark license agreements are defined as contracts which authorize the effective use by third parties of trademarks registered or deposited in Brazil, involving title to industrial property. Remuneration for such agreements is subject to treatment similar to patent license agreements. The legal period of validity for trademark license agreements is ten years.

Basic conditions unique to trademark license agreements are: (a) indication of whether license is exclusive or may be sublicensed; and (b) assurance that goods manufactured and services rendered under licensed trademarks shall be of the same quality as those rendered by licensor in home country. Other basic conditions are the same as for patent license agreements.

3. Industry technology license agreements are contracts which render available to the licensee the acquisition of know-how not protected by industrial property legislation, to be applied to the manufacturing of consumer goods and/or inputs in general. This know-how chiefly covers: (a) supply of all technical data of process or product engineering; (b) data required for upgrading product and/or process; and (c) transfer of technology compatible with current Brazilian policy of development of domestic technology which will contribute to improvement of the involved economic sector, leading to exportation of product. Licensed technology is also required to lead to replacement of imports of involved product.

Remuneration by licensee to licensor depends on the beginning of effective manufacturing of the product derived from the licensed technology. In establishing remuneration, to be considered are: (a) the degree of novelty and technical sophistication and quality of the licensed technology; (b) the willingness to update the licensed technology; (c) the R&D potential of the licensor; and (d) the estimated time period required for start-up operations. If remuneration for licensed technology has been previously established, it will be treated as a ceiling price, unless further negotiations occur. Terms of technology license agreements are limited to the time period required for the licensee to assimilate the licensor's technology. INPI has power to rule upon effective and appropriate technology utilization.

4. Technological and Industrial Cooperation Agreements are aimed at making available to the licensee the know-how involved in manufacturing industrial plants, machinery, equipment, etc. Remuneration for these agreements is based upon the same considerations as patent license agreements. Terms of the agreement may extend to a five-year period. The maximum amount of Brazilian engineering assistance is recommended.

5. Technical Service Agreements are contracted to plan, program, and perform studies and projects, and to render needed specialized services. Technical services performed on an ad hoc basis shall not exceed $20,000. Services covered by technical service agreements are: (a) preparation of urban development plans, feasibility, organizational and administrative studies; (b) preparation of engineering projects; (c)

installation, assembly and operation of machinery, equipment and industrial units; and (d) hiring non-resident technicians for specialized technical services. When possible, these technical services must be engaged through Brazilian engineering and/or consulting companies.

Remuneration for technical service agreements will be a fixed price based on costs incurred and the anticipated social benefit of the services. Non-residents shall not be remunerated as a percentage of gross earnings or production levels. Terms of technical service agreements are flexible.

INDEX